Anchored Hearts

Anchored Hearts

Healing Attachment Wounds Through God's Secure Love

Capt. Tony Newberry

Scripture quotations are from the Holy Bible, unless otherwise noted.

This book is for informational and inspirational purposes only. It is not intended to replace professional counseling, medical advice, diagnosis, or treatment. Readers are encouraged to seek appropriate professional guidance where necessary.

First Edition

Published independently by
Anchored Hearts Publishing

Cover design by Anthony Newberry
Interior design by Anthony Newberry

ISBN: 979-8-9953120-0-0

Printed in the United States of America

Dedication

First and always,
to my Lord and Savior, Jesus Christ.

You carried me through storms I did not see coming.
You stayed when I questioned everything.
You corrected me when I was wrong.
You steadied me when I was unraveling.

When my heart was breaking, You were not absent.
When I was learning hard lessons, You were not silent.
When I felt lost, You were already guiding me.

Every page of this book exists because You refused to let me drift.

To the love of my life.

You know who you are.

I did not write this book in spite of what we walked through.
I wrote it because of it.
I wrote it to help others through the pains we have both been through.

Loving you changed me.
Losing you changed me.
Missing you, every day, still changes me.

You awakened parts of my heart that had been guarded for years.
You exposed wounds I did not know were still shaping me.
You taught me depth, intensity, tenderness, and fear all at once.

I wish healing had come easier for both of us.
I wish we had understood sooner what we were carrying.
I wish the storms had not been louder than the truth.

I still believe what we had was real.
I still believe almost all relationships are salvageable when both hearts are willing.
I still pray that peace, clarity, and healing find you fully.

You are still loved more deeply than I ever said or showed well enough.

Yes, you are missed far more than these pages can express!

To you, the one holding this book.

If you are fighting for love, do it wisely.
If you are healing, do it honestly.
If you are confused, slow down before believing fear.

Do not let cognitive dissonance write the final chapter of something meaningful.
Do not surrender to narratives that feel protective but are not true.
Do not give up on growth where humility still exists.

May you regulate sooner.
May you repair quicker.
May you anchor deeper.
May you love with courage instead of control.

If this book helps you stay steady when everything in you wants to panic, then the storms that shaped it were not wasted.

— Capt. Tony —

Table of Contents

Preface viii

Introduction xvi

Chapter 1 – Designed for Connection 1

Chapter 2 – Understanding Attachment Styles 14

Chapter 3 – How God Responds to Our Attachment Patterns ... 29

Chapter 4 – How Attachment Shapes Our Lives Today 40

Chapter 5 – Why Attachment Patterns Are Hard to Break 51

Chapter 6 – How God Heals Attachment Wounds 63

Chapter 7 – Healing Together 75

Chapter 8 – Breaking Generational Cycles 90

Chapter 9 – When Love Is Tested 108

Chapter 10 – Living Securely 122

Chapter 11 – When Healing Leads to Reconciliation 134

Chapter 12 – Anchored Hearts 151

Epilogue 164

Acknowledgments

About the Author

Preface

Why This Book Had to Be Written

I did not set out to write a book about attachment.

I set out to understand why love can feel so strong and still feel so fragile.

For most of my life, I understood storms better than I understood emotions.

I knew how to read radar.
I knew how to calculate the tides.
I knew how to navigate channels in the dark.
I knew how to keep a vessel steady when the wind shifted unexpectedly.

But relationships?

That was a different situation to navigate.

I had seen love.
I believed in love.
I valued commitment.
I believed almost every relationship was worth fighting for.

Yet, I kept encountering something that confused me:

Two people could care deeply about each other and still hurt each other profoundly.

Two people could want the same future and still trigger each other's worst fears.

Two people could be committed and still feel unsafe.

It didn't make sense to me.

That is, until I began to understand attachment.

Attachment gave language to what I had been witnessing for years.

It explained why silence could feel like abandonment.
Why closeness could feel suffocating.
Why distance could feel catastrophic.
Why conflict could feel like collapse or failure.

It explained why some people pursue harder under stress while others withdraw to survive.

It explained why fear can rewrite narrative and why cognitive dissonance can convince us that something meaningful is meaningless or even scary or harmful.

Most importantly, it explained this:

Many relationships do not fail because love is absent.
They fail because safety has not yet been established.

That realization changed my view of so much in my life.

Not overnight.
Not perfectly.
But permanently.

I have lived enough life to know this:

We live in a culture that is far too quick to discard.

Quick to diagnose.
Quick to label incompatibility.
Quick to advise walking away.
Quick to say, "You deserve better," without ever asking whether growth is possible.

But I have also seen something else.

I have seen broken vessels rebuilt.

I have seen crews who once collided learn to coordinate.
I have seen marriages on the brink rediscover stability.
I have seen people confront their own patterns with humility and rebuild trust from the keel up.

I do not believe in walking away from someone simply because they struggle.

Mental illness is not disqualification.
Attachment insecurity is not disqualification.
Trauma is not disqualification.

Refusal to grow, that is different.

But struggle?
To struggle is human.

Most relationships are salvageable when both hearts are willing.

That conviction is not romantic optimism.

It was forged in real storms.

This book was not written from a place of superiority.

It was written from a place of humility.

I have activated.
I have misinterpreted.
I have allowed fear to speak louder than truth.

I have learned that strength is not control — it is regulation.

I have learned that secure love is not intensity — it is steadiness.

I have learned that reconciliation requires humility and work on **both** sides.

I have learned that sometimes wisdom requires release. A release that is not cold, quick, trigger-activated decision, but one that is a healthy and calculated boundary.

I have learned that God's steadiness is the only anchor that never shifts.

If this book feels grounded, it is because it was written from experience — not theory alone.

This book is written for believers who want to understand their attachment patterns through both Scripture and psychology.

It is for those who believe love is not disposable, that healing is possible, and that reconciliation should not be abandoned lightly.

It is for people who want to grow in emotional maturity without compromising biblical conviction.

If you are willing to look honestly at your patterns, and humbly at your faith, this book is for you.

I wrote this for:

The husband who feels misunderstood.
The wife who feels unseen.

The couple who loves deeply but keeps colliding.
The individual trying to break generational cycles.
The leader who wants to regulate instead of react.
The parent who wants to become the safe one.
The believer trying to reconcile psychology and faith.
The person sitting in silence wondering,

"Is this fixable?"

I wrote it because I believe healing changes legacy.

When one person regulates, generations shift.
When one person chooses repair over pride, culture changes.
When one person refuses to surrender to distorted narratives, relationships stabilize.

I wrote it because I believe love is worth fighting for — wisely, not blindly.

You will not find perfection in these pages.
You will find process.

You will not find condemnation.
You will find invitation.

You will not find a formula that eliminates storms.
You will find tools that help you anchor.

If you read this book carefully, you will see two themes woven throughout:

Security and reconciliation.

Security does not mean never feeling fear.
It means fear does not command your ship.

Reconciliation does not mean tolerating harm.
It means pursuing restoration where humility and safety exists.

Both require courage.

Both require regulation.

Both require truth.

Both require something larger than ourselves.

The sea has taught me something I will never forget:

Storms are not optional.
Preparation is.

This book is preparation.

Preparation for conflict.
Preparation for misunderstanding.
Preparation for cognitive distortion.
Preparation for seasons of distance.
Preparation for moments when fear whispers louder than truth.

Preparation to remain steady.

If you choose to walk through these chapters, I ask only one thing:

Read slowly.

Examine honestly.

Look not only at the other person's patterns — but at your own.

The goal of this book is not to prove someone wrong.

It is to build something stronger in **you**.

If, when you finish, you find yourself:

Pausing more.
Reacting less.
Repairing quicker.
Trusting deeper.
Releasing panic sooner.
Fighting wisely instead of impulsively.

Then it will have done what I hoped.

The sea will not grow quieter.

But you can grow steadier.

That steadiness changes everything.

— Capt. Tony —

INTRODUCTION

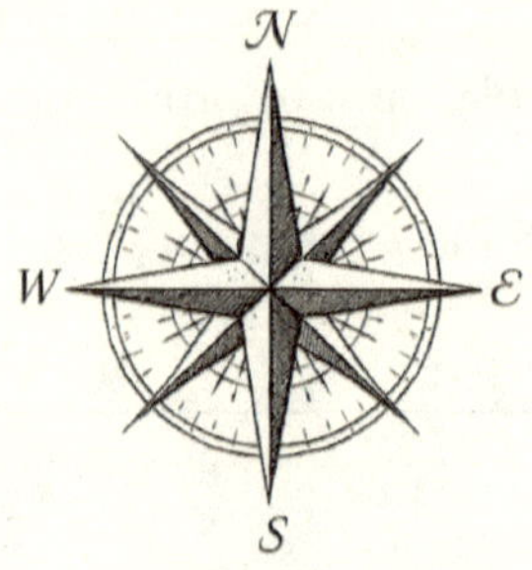

The Storm I Never Saw Coming

The sea has always made sense to me. It has always been the place where I find the most peace in this loud and crazy world.

People, on the other hand, have often been harder for me to understand.

Waves rise and fall with a kind of predictable rhythm. Storms gather, pass, and eventually give way to calmer waters. Currents shift continuously, but if you understand them, and use them to your advantage, they'll take you exactly where you want to go. If you know your instruments, your compass, your charts, your radar, you can navigate almost anything.

At least, that's what I believed for most of my life.

I've been the captain on vessels through nights so dark the horizon disappeared, and all I could see was the steady glow of the compass and electronics in front of me. I've felt the ocean rise beneath me like a living force, and I've watched lightning split the sky open. That's one of my favorite things to see — especially at night mid-ocean. I've heard the kind of wind that could make even seasoned sailors pray a little harder. Through all of it, I felt steady. Confident. On course. Anchored in my confidence.

However, nothing, not training, not seamanship, not experience, prepared me for the storm that developed in my own life.

If you have ever felt secure in love one moment and suddenly uncertain the next, you already understand the kind of storm this book explores.

The storm didn't come with strong winds and heavy seas.
It didn't roll in on dark clouds or rising wind.
It arrived quietly, in the ordinary rhythms of home.

Out of what felt like nowhere to me, there came a moment when the love of my life left and she wasn't coming home.

What I didn't yet understand was how much had been building beneath the surface — in both of us.

She wasn't gone forever — at least I didn't believe that she was then. I still believed we would work through it. I still believed our love would steady us.

But something had shifted.

What made it so disorienting was this: I had never thought I would lose her. Not once. Not for a single moment. We weren't a couple defined by constant conflict. There had been moments of distance, times she needed space while walking through deep things, times when I worked too hard and missed things in our home, moments of miscommunication or lack of communication, and times I didn't do the right things for her in our everyday life — but I believed we were secure. I believed what we had was steady. I always thought we had time to work on us.

So, when I understood she was moving out — that this wasn't just a difficult time but a real separation — something inside me gave way.

I remember standing in the doorway of our home, the room quiet in a way that didn't feel peaceful.

Sometimes silence is the loudest thing you can experience.

My chest felt tight — not like panic, but like pressure.

I didn't know what to do with myself. I wasn't angry.

I wasn't yelling.

I was stunned.

It felt like watching a vessel slowly drift from dock while still believing the lines were secure.

I kept thinking, "This will steady. We'll steady."

But underneath that thought was something deeper — fear I didn't yet have language for.

It wasn't anger.

It was shock — almost like a numbness protecting me.

I couldn't cry. I couldn't speak. I couldn't reach out for anyone. I just shut down within myself.

Beneath the shock was a question I had never considered:

What if I lose her for good?

For the first time in my life, I felt unanchored — not from the seafloor, but from certainty itself. From the future I thought was unfolding in front of us. From the quiet confidence that what we had was solid and safe and always would be.

My instinct wasn't to retreat.

It was to reach.
To fix it.
To steady it.
To hold on to something I felt suddenly slipping away.

I didn't have language then for this attachment or fear. I knew that I felt afraid in a way I had never felt before, and I knew that something I believed was secure suddenly felt so very fragile.

I knew how to command a vessel on the open sea…
but I didn't know how to command my own heart.

I knew how to manage a crew…
but I couldn't manage my own household.

I could interpret radar and read the water…
but I couldn't interpret what was happening inside me or in our home.

I could hold steady in a storm…
but I couldn't stop my inner world from totally collapsing.

The sea had rules…
life, it seemed, did not.

Yet, in that collapse, in the confusion, in the grief, in the unanswered questions, God met me in a way I had never experienced before.

Not with judgment, not with condemnation, not with a list of what I should have done differently.

He met me the way He met Elijah in the cave in 1 Kings 19:11-12…
with a whisper.

In that whisper, He began to show me something I had never truly understood:

Attachment

How we love.
How we fear.
How we bond.
How we lose.
How we heal.

He showed me that the patterns in my relationships, the way I clung, the way I feared loss, the way I tried to fix what wasn't mine to fix, weren't random. They were roots. They were old. Most importantly, they were calling for healing.

He showed me that the heart has currents, just like the sea — and if you don't understand them, they will carry you somewhere you never meant to go. That wounds have tides. That fear has a gravitational pull. That without an anchor, without Him, we drift uncontrollably.

In that whisper, He also showed me something even deeper:

His love is the only perfectly secure attachment we will ever have.
A love that does not abandon.
A love that does not withdraw.
A love that does not shame.
A love that does not break when life does.

This book is born from that journey.

It's about profound and deep heartbreak, yes.

More than that, it's about hope.

It's about discovering why we love the way we love.
It's about seeing ourselves with clarity and compassion.
It's about seeing others with this same clarity and compassion.
It's about letting ourselves be seen.
It's about learning to heal the wounds we didn't know we had — the ones we didn't cause but we still carry.
It's about letting God teach us the kind of secure love He designed us for from the beginning.

You don't have to be a captain to know what it feels like to be caught in a storm. You don't have to work on the water to know what it is to feel unanchored from yourself. Every one of us, at some point, encounters waves that threaten to take us under.

God doesn't leave us to drown; He steps into the storm; He speaks peace to the wind and waves as He did in Matthew 8:23-27. He invites us to anchor our hearts in Him, a love that is steady, safe, and unchanging. A love that is **secure.**

So, wherever you are in your journey, whether you feel anxious, avoidant, overwhelmed, disconnected, or simply tired, my prayer is that this book becomes a lighthouse for you.

Not pointing to me.
Not pointing to psychology alone.
But pointing to **Him**:
the God who heals attachment wounds,
the God who restores identity,
the God who remains when others leave,
the God who anchors us securely so we can love Him and love others well.

As you read, you will find many concepts and scriptures repeated. This isn't by accident but rather done so as I feel they are important to understanding and healing.

Welcome to *Anchored Hearts*.
Let's begin the healing together.

CHAPTER 1

Designed for Connection

Long before I ever studied attachment, trauma, or emotional patterns, I understood something else at a deep level:

The sea always tells the truth.

Waves don't pretend. Storms don't apologize. Currents don't hide their pull. The ocean is honest — even when it's unpredictable.

For most of my life, that honesty made sense to me.

I spent decades at sea as captain of party cruise boats, head boats, cruise ships, crewboats, supply vessels, core sample drill ships, tow boats, and tugs through waters around the world that demanded respect. The sea taught me discipline, humility, and the importance of knowing exactly where my vessel was, what lay ahead, and where my anchor was buried.

At sea, nothing stays hidden for long. If something is wrong with the vessel, the ocean exposes it. If the crew is fractured, it shows in their performance. If leadership is unstable, the whole ship feels it.

The sea reveals weaknesses.

My heartbreak revealed something deeper.

By the time my internal storm hit, I wasn't working away at sea anymore. I was home. I owned Island Cruises — a small passenger cruise vessel business in Carolina Beach, North Carolina. I was on the water every night, but never far from shore. I was building something rooted. Local. Beautiful.

We carried thousands of school children every year to our barrier islands to teach them about God's creation — many of them had never seen the ocean or been on a boat before.

We carried families down the Cape Fear River to watch sunsets melt into the horizon.

We carried partygoers under moonlight.

We launched the Christ Cruise — a free worship cruise where people encountered God on the water. On some of those cruises, we stopped at Masonboro Island and baptized people in warm coastal waters.

Outwardly, life felt settled.

Rooted.

Anchored.

That's what made what happened next so disorienting.

Because heartbreak doesn't require crashing waves.

It doesn't need wind or lightning.

It only needs one moment — the kind that quietly shifts certainty.

Suddenly, despite being surrounded by stability, I felt more exposed than I ever had on the open sea.

For the first time in my life, I realized I could navigate a vessel through a storm…

but I didn't know how to navigate my own heart through loss.

That realization began a journey that would take me somewhere far deeper than the ocean ever had.

Created for Connection

To understand healing, we must start at the beginning — not with our wounds, but with God's design.

Genesis is not just a creation account.

It is also a relational blueprint.

In Genesis 1, God creates light, land, ocean, sky, animals, and every form of life. After each act of creation, Scripture repeats the same phrase:

"And God saw that it was good."

Good.
Good.
Good.

Harmony.
Order.
Wholeness.

But then Genesis 2:18 interrupts the rhythm with this.

"It is not good for man to be alone."

Before sin.
Before shame.
Before fear.
Before trauma.

Aloneness is named as "not good."

This is staggering.

The first "not good" in the Bible is relational.

Human beings were not created merely to exist. We were created to connect.

God did not form Adam and say, "You have food, purpose, and oxygen — you'll be fine."

He said, "It is not good for you to be alone."

Why?

Because we reflect a relational God.

Father, Son, and Holy Spirit — a perfect union of love, connection, and mutual indwelling. We were created in that image. We carry within us a blueprint for belonging.

Connection is not weakness.

It is design.

A Biblical Story of Attachment Wound: Adam and Eve

Notice what happens immediately after sin enters the world — when Eve ate the fruit from the Tree of Knowledge of Good and Evil.

The first consequences are not famine or disease.
They are relational fractures.

Shame:
"They realized they were naked."
- Genesis 3:7

Fear:
"I was afraid."
- Genesis 3:10

Hiding:
"So I hid."
- Genesis 3:10

Blame:
"The woman You gave me…"
- Genesis 3:12

Deflection:
"The serpent deceived me, and I ate."
- Genesis 3:13

Connection shatters instantly.

Adam hides from God.
Adam blames Eve.
Eve blames the serpent.

The very first fracture in humanity is attachment-based.

We see relational fractures again and again throughout Scripture.

Elijah: The Prophet Who Felt Alone

In 1 Kings 18, Elijah performs one of the greatest miracles in Israel's history. Fire falls from heaven. False prophets are defeated.

Yet immediately afterward, in 1 Kings 19, he runs into the wilderness and says:

"I alone am left."

Objectively, that wasn't true.

But emotionally, it was.

Elijah collapses under isolation.

He doesn't need more power.
He doesn't need more miracles.

He needs reassurance of connection.

How does God respond?

Not with thunder.
Not with fire.
Not with spectacle.

With a whisper.

The God who designed attachment heals through presence.

A Captain's Lesson in Isolation

Years ago, on a long overseas assignment, I watched a strong young deckhand slowly change.

At the dock, he was confident, jovial, and outgoing.
At sea, he became withdrawn.
Short-tempered.
Quiet.

Weeks away from family.
Stuck in confined quarters.
Riding through varying sea states.
Having limited emotional outlet.

At a time before high-speed internet at sea, isolation from his loved ones reshaped him.

Nothing dramatic happened.

No explosion.
No fight.

Just slow relational deprivation.

When we finally docked in Chaguaramas, Trinidad, and we were set to crew change home, he told me something I never forgot:

"Captain, I didn't realize how much I needed my people until I didn't have them. I don't think I'm cut out for this life."

That was the end of his career at sea. I never saw him again.

We are not built for isolation.

Yet many of us learned early that connection is unsafe.

How Attachment Forms

Attachment styles are not personality quirks.

They are survival adaptations.

- Secure attachment forms when love is consistent.
- Anxious attachment forms when love is inconsistent.
- Avoidant attachment forms when love is emotionally distant.

- Disorganized attachment forms when love and fear are mixed together.

A young child does not choose these patterns.

They absorb them.

They learn:

Is closeness safe?
Is distance safer?
Is vulnerability punished?
Is independence required?
Is love stable?

These questions and answers form beneath conscious awareness.

They follow us into adulthood.

Into dating.
Into marriage.
Into parenting.
Into ministry.
Into faith.

Attachment becomes the invisible current beneath every relationship.

A Fictitious Story

Imagine a little boy who runs to his mother every time he's scared.

Sometimes she picks him up.

Sometimes she says, "You're fine."

Sometimes she's overwhelmed.

Sometimes she's warm.

He learns something, but he doesn't know he's learning it.

He learns to scan.
To monitor.
To cling.
To over-explain.
To anticipate.

Fast forward twenty-five years.

He falls deeply in love.

The first time his partner pulls away emotionally, something inside him panics.

He doesn't think, "This is my attachment style."

He thinks, "I'm losing her."

He reaches harder.
Calls more.
Explains more.
Tries to fix more.

He's not controlling.

He's terrified.

He doesn't know he's reliving something much older.

This is how attachment works.

It is rarely about the present moment alone.

Why This Matters for You — And For Me

When my own heartbreak hit, it revealed something I had never examined:

My attachment patterns.
My fear of loss.
My instinct to reach.
My urgency to fix.

None of those things were sinful.
They were shaped.

If we don't examine what shaped us and seek healing where we need it, we will repeat it – and likely pass it on to those who come after us.

God Did Not Abandon the Design

The story does not end in Genesis 3.

Throughout Scripture, God reattaches Himself to His people.

He pursues.
He reassures.
He remains.

Romans 8 says nothing can separate us from the love of God.

Psalm 34:18 says, "He is close to the brokenhearted…"

Remember this. I will repeat it throughout this book as it is profound!

Jesus calms storms not just on water — but in people.

Secure attachment begins vertically — in a relationship with a God who does not withdraw.

When the heart learns that God does not withdraw,
does not abandon,
does not shame,
does not panic,
does not leave.

It slowly begins to heal.

Closing This Chapter

We were designed for connection.

Not isolation.
Not survival.
Not emotional self-protection.

Connection.

When that connection breaks, the heart feels it.

But the same God who designed attachment also restores it.

In the chapters ahead, we'll go deeper:

- into biblical figures and their attachment patterns
- into how these dynamics shape relationships today
- into how secure love is rebuilt

- into how God anchors what once drifted

God does not leave us stranded.

Shame fractured connection.
Fear distorted it.

God restores it.
He begins with connection.

CHAPTER 2

Understanding Attachment Styles

If you've ever watched several boats riding through the same seas and responding differently, you already understand something about attachment.

One vessel moves steady through the chop.
Another struggles heavily with every wave.
Another keeps its distance from the harbor, avoiding the crowd.
Another drifts unpredictably — engine surging, then stalling — because something inside its systems is damaged.

The water may be the same.
The responses? They are not.

People are like that too.

Two people can experience the same disagreement, the same silence, the same moment of tension — and respond completely differently.

One steadies.
One pursues.
One withdraws.
One panics and shuts down.

Attachment is the set of patterns your heart learned — often very early in childhood, often quietly — about connection:

Is love safe?
Will people stay?
What happens when I need something?
What do I do when closeness feels threatened?
What do I do when emotions rise?

Psychology calls these patterns "attachment styles," but Scripture has been revealing the dynamics of fear, connection, pursuit, withdrawal, and restoration for thousands of years.

This chapter is not about labeling people.
It is about understanding the currents beneath our reactions so healing can begin where it matters most — in relationship with God and with the safe people around us.

Most of us are not one pure category. We are a blend. However, under stress, most of us lean in one direction.

Stress exposes attachment the way storms expose a vessel's weaknesses.

Let's walk through the four primary attachment styles — secure, anxious, avoidant (dismissive), and disorganized (fearful) — with compassion, clarity, and hope.

Secure Attachment — Steady Love, Safe Connection

Secure attachment is the blueprint.

It forms when love is experienced as consistent, emotionally safe, and responsive. A securely attached person is not someone who never struggles. It is someone who, deep down, believes connection is trustworthy — even when it is tested.

Secure attachment sounds like:

- "We can work through this."
- "Conflict doesn't mean abandonment."
- "I can express my needs."
- "I am worthy of love."
- "You can be upset with me and still stay."

A Biblical Picture of Secure Attachment: Jesus

Jesus embodied secure attachment.

He loved deeply — but did not cling.
He set boundaries — but did not shame.
He withdrew to pray — but always returned.
He wept — but was not consumed by panic.

When Peter denied Him, Jesus did not retaliate. He restored him.

Secure attachment is what love looks like when fear is not steering.

Scripture says:

"Perfect love casts out fear."
— 1 John 4:18

Fear may whisper, but it does not command the vessel.

What Secure Looks Like in Real Life

I've watched seasoned captains in heavy weather.

The inexperienced captain oversteers, reacting to every swell.
The seasoned one adjusts — not dramatically — but steadily.

He doesn't ignore the storm.
He doesn't panic at it either.

He trusts the vessel.
He trusts the crew.
He trusts what he feels.

Secure attachment feels like that.

Not storm-free.
Not emotionless.
Just steady.

Secure attachment can be learned. Through repeated experiences of safe love — especially with God and with safe people — the nervous system can learn what safety feels like.

That is hopeful.

Because no matter where you begin, secure is possible.

Anxious Attachment — When Love Feels Uncertain

Anxious attachment often forms when love was inconsistent.

Warm one day.
Distant the next.
Present sometimes.
Unavailable at critical moments.

The child learns:

"I have to work to keep love close."

The nervous system becomes alert to signs of distance. It scans for tone shifts. It watches for pauses. It feels the slightest change.

Anxious attachment often sounds like:

- "Are you upset with me?"
- "Why haven't you responded?"
- "Did I do something wrong?"
- "Please don't leave."
- "If I can just fix this, we'll be okay."

Anxious people are often deeply loving and loyal. But when closeness feels threatened, fear takes the wheel.

Biblical Picture of Anxious Attachment: Peter

Peter loved Jesus intensely.

When Jesus spoke of leaving, Peter reacted strongly.
When Jesus was arrested, Peter followed — then panicked.
When he failed, he wept bitterly.

Peter was not weak. He was attached.

His fear was not a lack of devotion — it was devotion mixed with fear of loss.

Jesus did not shame him. He restored him beside a fire and asked, "Do you love me?," three times.

Healing for the anxious heart is not "be less needy." Healing is learning felt safety — reassurance that does not withdraw.

A Story to Recognize

Imagine a woman who grew up with a father who traveled frequently. Sometimes he called. Sometimes he didn't. When he did, he was warm. When he didn't, she felt invisible.

She learns to anticipate. To monitor. To over-explain.

As an adult, when her husband grows quiet after a long day, her body registers danger.

She asks, "Are we okay?"
He says, "Of course."
But her body does not settle.

She texts again later. Then again.

She is not trying to control.

She is trying to steady herself.

Anxious attachment is not weakness.
It is love afraid of losing what matters.

Avoidant Attachment
When Vulnerability Feels Unsafe

Avoidant attachment often forms when emotional closeness was discouraged or dismissed.

"Stop crying."
"You're fine."
"Handle it yourself."
"Toughen up."

The child learns:

"My needs are too much."
"Independence is safer than closeness."

Avoidant attachment often sounds like:

- "I'm fine."
- "It's not a big deal."
- "I don't want to talk about it."
- "I need space."

Avoidant individuals often appear strong and composed. Yet most avoidant hearts feel deeply — they simply learned that vulnerability brings discomfort or rejection.

Biblical Picture of Avoidant Attachment: Jonah

God calls Jonah.
Jonah runs.

Not because he lacks belief.
Because proximity feels overwhelming.

He withdraws.
He distances.
He numbs.

God does not chase Jonah with shame.
He pursues him patiently — even through a storm.

Avoidant attachment is not coldness.

It is protection.

A Story to Recognize

Imagine a man raised in a home where emotions were inconvenient.

When conflict arose, his parents went silent.

As an adult, when his wife raises concerns, his body tightens. He does not yell. He does not explode.

He shuts down.

He feels flooded but cannot name it.

He withdraws to calm himself, but she feels abandoned.

He is not cold.

He is overwhelmed.

Avoidant attachment is protection, not indifference.

Disorganized Attachment
When Love and Fear Are Entangled

Disorganized attachment forms when safety and fear are intertwined.

The caregiver is both comfort and threat.

The child learns:

"I need you."
"But you scare me."

Closeness becomes confusing. The nervous system receives mixed signals — move toward, pull away, brace for impact.

Disorganized attachment often looks like:

- Intense closeness followed by sudden withdrawal
- Emotional flooding followed by numbness
- Fear of abandonment mixed with fear of intimacy
- Shame after reactions

Biblical Picture of Disorganized Attachment: David

David trusted God deeply.

Yet David also made impulsive, destructive decisions — especially in moments of relational vulnerability.

His longing for connection and his fear-driven choices coexisted.

He wrote psalms of desperation and repentance. He oscillated between confidence and collapse.

He was not unstable because he lacked faith.

He was human.

Disorganized attachment is often trauma-based. It is not drama. It is a nervous system that never learned what safety feels like.

A Story to Recognize

Imagine a woman who grew up in a home where love came with volatility.

Sometimes her mother was warm.
Sometimes explosive.

As an adult, when someone gets close, she feels relief — and panic.

She leans in.
Then pulls back.
Then apologizes.
Then distances again.

She hates this pattern, but her body learned early that closeness and danger live in the same place.

Disorganized attachment is not chaos for chaos' sake.

It is a heart longing for safety but unsure how to receive it.

Recognizing Your Pattern

Before we talk about healing, pause here.

Ask yourself:

When conflict arises, do I move toward or away?
When someone grows quiet, do I feel anxious, relieved, or confused?
Do I fear abandonment more, or do I fear being overwhelmed more?

Do I over-explain and over-reach — or minimize and shut down?
Do I long for closeness but panic once it arrives?
How do I respond to God's silence? With trust, fear, distance, or confusion?

You do not need to diagnose yourself perfectly.

You only need to become aware.

Awareness is not accusation.
It is clarity.
Clarity is where healing begins.

Where These Patterns Come From

Attachment styles form through repeated relational experiences. Often beginning before you had even learned to speak.

Not one moment.
Patterns.

Your attachment style is not a moral failure.
It is an adaptation.
A strategy.
A survival map.

These survival maps are not always healthy relationship maps.

Sometimes what served you when you were younger no longer does as you grow.

Healing means updating the map.

How This Touched My Own Life

When heartbreak exposed my own attachment patterns, I realized something uncomfortable:

My instinct was to reach harder.
To fix faster.
To steady what felt unstable.

I was mostly secure — but I had anxious traits, especially when under stress.

The fear was not simply about a moment.
It was about losing connection.

That instinct was not sinful.
It was shaped.

Until we understand what shaped us, we will react from it instead of healing through it.

You have to get to the core of the attachment and work from there.

That realization changed the direction of my journey.

The Hope

Every attachment pattern can move toward secure.

Not through willpower.
Not through shame.
Through consistent, safe love.

That begins vertically — with a God who does not withdraw, shame, panic, or abandon.

Secure attachment begins when the heart experiences repeated safety.

Over time, fear loosens.
The nervous system settles.
The ship steadies.

Closing Image

Imagine four ships approaching harbor:

Secure docks with calm adjustments.
Anxious circles, worried about aligning with the dock.
Avoidant lingers offshore.
Disorganized moves forward, then pulls back.

The harbor does not reject any of them.

It remains steady.

That is what God is.

Steady.

From that steadiness, healing begins.

Attachment Styles at a Glance

Secure
Core belief: I am worthy of love and others are generally trustworthy.

Core fear: Temporary loss of connection.
Growth path: Continue choosing vulnerability and repair.

Anxious
Core belief: I must pursue to preserve connection.
Core fear: Abandonment.
Growth path: Regulate before pursuing. Learn to tolerate temporary distance.

Avoidant
Core belief: I must rely on myself to stay safe.
Core fear: Loss of autonomy or engulfment.
Growth path: Stay present when discomfort rises. Practice safe vulnerability.

Disorganized
Core belief: Love feels unpredictable and unsafe.
Core fear: Both abandonment and closeness.
Growth path: Build consistent safety with God and regulated relationships.

CHAPTER 3

How God Responds to Our Attachment Patterns

Scripture tells the truth about the human heart.

It does not airbrush fear.
It does not tidy up insecurity.
It does not present flawless heroes.

Instead, it gives us people — people who loved God deeply and still wrestled with anxiety, withdrawal, shame, intensity, collapse, and confusion.

The Bible reveals something remarkable:

God does not withdraw from insecure attachment patterns.
He moves toward them.

If Chapter 2 helped you recognize your patterns, this chapter helps you see how God responds to them.

Attachment is not only about how we react.
It is about how love reacts to us.

When Fear Fears Losing Love — Peter

Peter loved Jesus with intensity.

He left everything quickly.
He stepped out of a boat into open water.
He declared loyalty even unto death.
He was bold.
He was devoted.
He was impulsive.

He was also afraid.

When Jesus spoke of suffering and leaving, Peter rebuked Him.
When soldiers came to arrest Him, Peter drew a sword.

When pressure mounted in the courtyard, Peter denied Him.

Not because he stopped loving.
Because he feared losing the One he loved.

Anxious attachment is not shallow devotion.
It is deep devotion mixed with fear of separation.

After the resurrection, Jesus did not replay Peter's failure publicly.
He did not shame him in front of the others.
He recreated the scene — a charcoal fire — and asked gently:

"Do you love Me?"
— John 21:15

Three times.

Not to reopen the wound.
To heal it.

Jesus restored Peter at the point of his shame.

Fear expected distance.
Love moved closer.

Anxious hearts expect rejection when they fail. Secure love refuses to withdraw. That refusal begins to retrain fear. The nervous system learns that closeness does not disappear under pressure.

Peter's fear did not disqualify him.
It became the place where restoration began.

When Exhaustion Feels Like Abandonment — Elijah

Elijah's collapse in 1 Kings 19 often gets summarized too quickly.

In the previous chapter, fire had fallen from heaven.
False prophets were defeated.
God's power was undeniable.

One chapter later, Elijah runs into the wilderness and says:

"I have had enough."
"I am no better than my ancestors."
"I am the only one left."
— 1 Kings 19:4, 10

Exhaustion distorts perception.
Isolation amplifies fear.
An overwhelmed nervous system often interprets temporary silence as abandonment.

God's response is revealing.

He does not rebuke Elijah for weak faith.
He does not lecture him about perspective.

He lets him sleep.
He feeds him.
He restores his body before addressing his theology.

Only after rest does God speak — and He speaks in a whisper.

Secure attachment often begins with regulation before revelation.

God steadies Elijah physically, then emotionally, then spiritually. Safety comes before instruction. Calm precedes correction.

Fear says, "I am alone."
God replies, gently, "You are not."

Anxious hearts do not heal through shame. They heal through consistent reassurance that does not disappear when strength falters.

When Love Carries Grief — Martha

Female readers deserve to see themselves clearly in these pages. Martha offers that mirror.

In John 11, Lazarus is dying. Martha sends word to Jesus. He delays. Lazarus dies.

When Jesus arrives, Martha meets Him with a mixture of faith and disappointment:

"Lord, if You had been here, my brother would not have died."
— John 11:21

Those words carry attachment tension.

She believes in Him.
She trusts Him.
She also feels hurt.

Martha is not hysterical.
She is grieving.

She holds belief and disappointment in the same breath.

Jesus does not shame her honesty.
He does not minimize her grief.
He does not say, "You should have trusted more."

He invites her deeper:

"I am the resurrection and the life."
— John 11:25

Secure attachment grows when disappointment can be voiced safely. God does not punish emotional honesty. He engages it.

Martha's grief was not faithlessness. It was attachment under strain.

Jesus meets her in conversation, not condemnation. Safety is strengthened through relational engagement.

When Proximity Feels Overwhelming — Jonah

Jonah's story often gets reduced to disobedience. The deeper layer reveals emotional avoidance.

God calls Jonah to Nineveh — a city marked by violence and moral corruption. The assignment is heavy. The emotional weight is real.

Jonah does not debate theology.
He runs.

Avoidant patterns often activate when closeness or responsibility feels overwhelming.

Jonah boards a ship headed in the opposite direction.
He sleeps during the storm.
He withdraws from engagement.

Shutdown can look calm on the outside while chaos churns beneath the surface.

God does not erase Jonah.
He interrupts him.

A storm.
A confrontation.
A fish.

Again — not punishment — interruption.

Avoidant hearts are not healed through cornering. They are healed through patient pursuit that refuses to disappear.

Even inside the fish, God remains present. Even after Nineveh repents, God continues speaking to Jonah. Questions replace condemnation.

Avoidant attachment says, "Distance is safer."
Secure love says, "I will remain steady even when you pull away."

Consistency over time softens avoidance. Presence that does not pressure creates space for re-engagement.

When Love and Fear Are Entangled — David

David's life carries the marks of trauma.

Overlooked by his father.
Sent alone into danger.
Pursued by a jealous king.
Forced into caves and exile.

Safety and threat coexisted in his formative years. That mixture often produces **disorganized** attachment.

David's Psalms swing between:

"The Lord is my shepherd; I shall not want."
— Psalm 23:1

and

"My God, why have You forsaken me?"
— Psalm 22:1

Confidence and collapse live side by side.
Longing for connection and fear of betrayal coexist.

In relationships, David shows devotion and destructive impulse. Intimacy and self-sabotage sit uncomfortably close.

Disorganized attachment often carries the belief:

"Something is wrong with me."

David's life tells a different story.

Correction comes.
Consequences come.
Presence remains.

Disorganized attachment heals when consistency outlasts chaos.

God anchors David repeatedly. Covenant remains intact even when behavior falters. Steadiness interrupts instability.

Love does not disappear when the heart feels conflicted.

A Woman with a History — The Samaritan Woman

In John 4, Jesus meets a woman at a well.

Five husbands.
A current relationship outside marriage.
A noon visit to avoid the crowd.

Relational instability marks her story. Shame likely trails her steps.

Jesus does not expose her publicly.
He does not rehearse her failures.
He names her history gently and continues the conversation.

He offers living water.

Attachment wounds often lead to repeated relational patterns. Jesus addresses the thirst beneath the behavior.

Secure love identifies the need beneath the pattern.

She leaves the well transformed — not because she was condemned, but because she was seen.

Secure attachment begins when being fully known does not result in rejection.

Jesus — Secure Attachment in Human Form

Every biblical character reveals insecure attachment patterns.

Jesus reveals secure attachment embodied.

He loves without clinging.
He sets boundaries without hostility.
He withdraws to pray and returns to relationship.
He weeps without losing composure.
He confronts without humiliating.

His security flows from uninterrupted connection with the Father.

Secure attachment is not independence.
It is rooted dependence on a love that does not shift.

Jesus demonstrates:

Presence without panic.
Closeness without control.
Distance without abandonment.
Truth without cruelty.

He is not merely a model.
He is the anchor.

When we attach to Him, our nervous systems encounter something different — a love that does not escalate, disappear, or destabilize under stress.

Repeated exposure to that steadiness begins to heal what fear shaped.

The Pattern Beneath the Stories

Across Scripture, a pattern emerges:

Fear expects rejection.
God offers presence.

Shame expects exposure.
God offers covering.

Withdrawal expects distance.
God pursues.

Chaos expects abandonment.
God remains.

Every insecure pattern meets secure love.

That thread runs through Scripture.
That thread runs through your story.

Where This Leads

The next chapter turns from Scripture to daily life.

Patterns rarely live alone.
They collide in relationships.

Anxious meets avoidant.
Secure meets insecure.
Disorganized meets stability.

Understanding the pattern is awareness.
Experiencing secure love is healing.

Healing does not begin with perfection.
It begins with attachment to a God who remains steady.

From that steadiness, the heart relearns what it was designed for:

Connection without fear.

CHAPTER 4

How Attachment Shapes Our Lives Today

By now, you may be starting to recognize yourself.

Maybe you saw your heart in Peter's fear of abandonment.
Maybe you recognized your exhaustion in Elijah's collapse.
Maybe Jonah's withdrawal felt uncomfortably familiar.
Maybe David's emotional swings sounded like your own inner world.

Recognition is not coincidence.

It is clarity.

Attachment does not stay in childhood.

It does not remain buried in early memories.

It does not disappear when we grow older, become Christians, start dating, get married, build businesses, or raise children.

Attachment travels with us.

I have watched captains bring old bad habits on to new vessels. A captain can upgrade their boat, improve their electronics, add stabilizers, hire better crew — yet still manage the crew the same poor way they always have and end up with the same lackluster results.

The ocean may change.
The equipment may improve.
The leadership patterns may remain.

That same thing happens in relationships.

We upgrade our circumstances.

We keep our old responses.

The same old patterns continue.

The Sea May Change — The Steering Often Doesn't

At sea, what determines a vessel's response is rarely the water alone.

Two boats can enter the same inlet under the same sea state and experience entirely different outcomes.

One captain reads the current early and compensates before tension builds.
Another reacts late and fights the tide.

One trusts the chart and makes measured corrections.
Another doubts the instruments and second-guesses every movement.

One grips the wheel too tightly and misses the feel of the vessel.
Another lets the wind decide.

The conditions may be identical.

The internal calibration is not.

Every vessel carries a hidden system beneath the deck — cables, hydraulics, electronics — translating small movements of the wheel into larger directional shifts.

When that system is aligned, steering feels smooth and measured.

When it isn't, even minor adjustments create inconsistent or unexpected turns.

Attachment functions the same way.

It is the unseen calibration system of the heart.

It determines:

- how quickly we brace
- how intensely we interpret
- how much threat we detect
- how strongly we pursue or retreat
- how steady we remain when connection wavers

Most of us assume we are responding to the present moment.

In truth, we are often responding to an old imprint — an internal warning that says:

Danger is coming. Protect the bond. Protect yourself.

The sea does not always create instability.

Sometimes it just reveals instability that was already there.

Relationships do the same.

Attachment Is the Lens, Not the Moment

One of the most important truths in this chapter is simple:

Attachment is not about the event.

It is about the meaning your nervous system assigns to the event.

Two people experience the same silence.

One thinks, "They must be busy."
Another thinks, "I'm about to be abandoned."

Two people receive the same feedback.

One thinks, "That helps."
Another thinks, "I'm not enough."

Two people experience space.

One feels calm.
Another feels panic.
Another feels relief.

The moment is identical.

The interpretation is not.

Attachment is the lens.

When Attachment Collides

The most revealing place attachment shows up is not in isolation.

It shows up in collision.

Anxious meets avoidant.
Secure meets insecure.
Disorganized meets stability.

Picture a narrow inlet with shifting currents.

One captain wants to move quickly before the tide turns.
Another wants to wait until conditions feel safer.

Both believe they are protecting the vessel.

Many relationships unfold the same way.

In recent years, many people encountering these painful patterns have reached for a quick explanation — one word that seems to make sense of everything:

Narcissism.

But that word is often used far more quickly than it should be.

When "Narcissism" Becomes the Wrong Diagnosis

In modern conversations about relationships, the word *narcissist* appears everywhere.

Social media uses it.
Friends use it.
Breakups are often explained with it.

Sometimes the label is accurate.

Much more often, it is not.

Today, almost any painful relationship dynamic risks being summarized with one conclusion:

"They're a narcissist."

But real narcissism is far more complex than that.

Clinical narcissism involves persistent patterns such as:

- grandiose self-importance
- chronic need for admiration
- lack of empathy
- manipulation for personal gain
- entitlement
- inability to take responsibility for harm

These traits are not occasional behaviors.

They are deeply rooted personality structures that show up consistently across many relationships and situations.

Most difficult relational behavior is **not narcissism**.

Attachment activation can create behaviors that look selfish or defensive on the surface.

An *avoidant* partner may withdraw during conflict. Leaving their partner feeling ignored, used, or abandoned.

An *anxious* partner may pursue reassurance intensely. Leaving their partner feeling smothered, pressured, or controlled.

A *disorganized* partner may swing between closeness and distance. Leaving their partner confused entirely.

These responses can hurt deeply.

But hurt does not automatically equal narcissism.

Attachment reactions are often attempts by the nervous system to regulate fear.

A person shutting down may not lack empathy.
They may feel overwhelmed.

A person pursuing reassurance may not be controlling.
They may be afraid of abandonment.

When these patterns are misunderstood, people sometimes assume malicious intent where there is actually fear.

A Story of Mislabeling

A couple once described their relationship to me this way.

She said quietly, "I think he's a narcissist."

Her voice carried exhaustion.

For years, she had tried to talk through conflict. When tension rose, he withdrew. When she pushed for answers, he shut down further.

Eventually she began reading articles and watching videos online about narcissistic partners.

Many of the descriptions sounded familiar.

Withdrawal.
Defensiveness.
Avoiding emotional conversations.

So, the label seemed to fit.

But when the situation slowed down and the patterns were examined more carefully, something different became clear.

He was not manipulating.
He was not seeking admiration.
He was not exploiting her.

He was overwhelmed.

When conflict intensified, his nervous system treated it like danger.

His instinct was not domination — it was escape.

He had learned early in life that emotional conflict often led to criticism and shame.

Silence had been the safest option.

So, when pressure rose in adulthood, he shut down.

What she experienced as indifference was actually fear.

What she experienced as narcissism was actually avoidance.

Understanding this did not immediately solve their relationship.
But it changed the conversation.

Instead of "You don't care about me," the language shifted toward:

"When you go quiet, I feel alone."

Instead of "You're manipulating me," the conversation became:

"When things escalate, I feel overwhelmed and shut down."

The moment the label disappeared, curiosity returned.

That curiosity is where healing begins.

Narcissism Is Not an Attachment Style

This distinction is important.

Attachment styles describe how the nervous system organizes connection and safety.

They are patterns learned through early relational experiences.

Narcissism, by contrast, is a personality disorder involving identity structure, empathy deficits, and chronic relational dysfunction.

Attachment insecurity can often improve through:

- awareness
- safe relationships
- therapy
- spiritual growth
- emotional regulation

True narcissistic pathology is far more resistant to change.

Confusing the two can lead people to give up on relationships that may still contain humility, empathy, and the potential for growth.

Discernment matters.

Sometimes what looks like narcissism is actually unhealed attachment reacting under stress.

Sometimes it is not.

Wisdom requires the patience to tell the difference.

The Anxious – Avoidant Dance

Imagine a couple at the end of a long day.

She says quietly, "We need to talk."

His shoulders tense. He hears criticism coming.

Her chest tightens. She already feels him pulling away.

She moves toward him emotionally.

He creates space physically.

She says, "Why are you shutting down?"

He says, "Why are you making this a big deal?"

She feels abandonment.

He feels invasion.

Neither is trying to hurt the other.

Both are steering from fear.

The anxious heart is trying to prevent loss.

The avoidant heart is trying to prevent overwhelm.

Without awareness, they trigger each other repeatedly.

With awareness, they begin to see that the conflict is not the enemy.

The fear beneath it is.

Secure Attachment in Daily Life

Secure adults are not emotionless.

They feel deeply.
They react.
They get hurt.
They get frustrated.

The difference is regulation.

A secure captain in rough water does not ignore the storm.
He adjusts without losing composure.
He does not overcorrect.
He does not abandon the wheel.

Securely attached adults tend to:

- stay present during disagreement
- repair after conflict
- tolerate emotional discomfort
- trust that love can survive tension
- ask for what they need without panic
- allow others to have feelings without assuming abandonment

Security is not perfection.

It is steadiness.

Security says, "This wave does not mean the ship is sinking."

CHAPTER 5

Why Attachment Patterns Are So Hard to Break

Once you begin to recognize your attachment patterns, a natural question follows:

"If I can see it, why can't I stop it?"

Why do you still react the same way, even when you know better?
Why does your heart race before your thoughts organize?
Why do old fears surface in new relationships?
Why does distance still ache so deeply — or closeness still feel overwhelming?

Awareness brings clarity.
Clarity often brings frustration.

Because insight alone does not create change.

The reason is both simple and profound:

Attachment patterns do not live in your thoughts.
They actually live in your nervous system.

The Reaction That Beats Your Reasoning

On the bridge of a vessel, reaction time matters.

If a squall line builds quickly, the body responds before the brain finishes calculating wind speed. Hands move to throttle. Eyes scan instruments. Muscles tighten. Your body feels it before your mind processes what it is receiving.

That reaction is not weakness.
It is training.

Your nervous system works the same way.

When attachment feels threatened, your body reacts before logic speaks. The chest tightens. The stomach drops. The jaw clenches. Breathing shifts. Tone changes. Words sharpen or disappear.

You may tell yourself, "This isn't a big deal."

Your body may disagree.

This is not intellectual.
It is physiological.
Your body remembers what your mind has forgotten.

Attachment Is Learned Before Language

Most attachment patterns formed before you had words to explain what you felt.

Before memory.
Before reasoning.
Before theology.
Before choice.

They formed while your brain was still wiring itself around safety and threat.

Your nervous system learned:

- This is what connection feels like.
- This is what danger feels like.
- This is how I survive.

That learning did not require intention.
It required repetition.

If love felt inconsistent, your body learned vigilance.

If emotion felt overwhelming, your body learned distance.

If comfort and fear came from the same source, your body learned confusion.

Once the nervous system encodes a pattern, it does not politely ask whether the pattern is still necessary.

It activates it.

Why Willpower Fails

Many people attempt to heal attachment wounds through effort.

"I will be less needy."
"I will stop overthinking."
"I will just open up."
"I will not shut down."

Effort targets behavior.
Attachment lives beneath behavior.

Willpower can override reaction briefly.
It cannot retrain fear by force.

Fear does not respond to lectures.
Fear responds to safety.

This tension is not new.

Paul writes:

"I do not understand what I do. For what I want to do I do not do, but what I hate I do."
— Romans 7:15

That is not spiritual incompetence.
It is human wiring.

I remember realizing that knowing my attachment pattern did not stop it from activating.

Insight did not calm my body.

Scripture, I had memorized did not immediately slow my pulse.

That was humbling.

I could navigate a vessel through rough weather.
I could not always regulate my own internal storm.

That realization forced me to approach healing differently.

You can want to react differently and still feel pulled by something deeper.

The pull is not moral failure.
It is neural patterning.

The Survival System

When attachment feels threatened, the nervous system shifts into survival modes.

Fight — control, anger, intensity.
Flight — withdrawal, distance, avoidance.
Freeze — numbness, shutdown, silence.
Fawn — appeasing, over-accommodating, losing yourself to keep peace.

Each response once protected you.

At some point in your story, those reactions reduced pain.

A child who scanned for tone shifts stayed prepared.
A child who stayed quiet avoided escalation.
A child who pleased survived unpredictability.

The nervous system does not forget what once worked.

It simply repeats it.

Even when it no longer serves you and may actually be harming you.

Familiar Pain Versus Unfamiliar Peace

One of the most uncomfortable truths in attachment healing is this:

The nervous system prefers familiar pain to unfamiliar peace.

Not because pain feels good.
But, because it feels known.

Predictable instability can feel safer than unfamiliar calm.

If chaos marked your early experiences, steadiness could feel suspicious.

If emotional intensity once meant connection, quiet safety could feel empty.

If distance protected you, closeness may feel intrusive.

Not wrong.
Unfamiliar.

The Spiritual Layer

Attachment patterns shape how you experience God.

An anxious heart may pray urgently and interpret silence as distance or abandonment.

An avoidant heart may believe deeply yet resist intimacy.

A disorganized heart may love God intensely while feeling unworthy of His love.

Faith does not erase attachment patterns.
It reveals them.

God does not bypass the nervous system.

He enters it.

"Perfect love casts out fear."
— 1 John 4:18

Fear is not argued away.
It is displaced by consistent, safe love.

Repeated exposure to a God who remains steady begins to retrain internal alarms.

Not instantly.
Gradually.

Shame Makes the Pattern Stronger

Many believers respond to recurring attachment reactions with shame.

"I should be past this."

"I know better."

"Why am I still like this?"

Shame adds threat to an already activated system.

When shame enters, the nervous system hears:

"You are unsafe even within yourself."

That reinforces hypervigilance.

Correction without compassion deepens wiring.

God does not heal through humiliation.

Throughout Scripture, conviction leads to restoration, not rejection.

Shame says, "Hide."

Secure love says, "Stay."

Healing cannot occur in hiding.

Repatterning Takes Repetition

At sea, when you adjust course, the vessel does not turn instantly.
There is resistance.
Momentum continues in the old direction for a moment before the heading responds.

Attachment healing works the same way.

Insight is the turn of the wheel.
Repetitive correction of the heading is what changes the course towards new destinations.

Each time you stay present instead of withdrawing, a new pathway strengthens.

Each time you regulate before reacting, safety grows.

Each time you experience conflict without abandonment, the nervous system updates its map.

Change does not occur through intensity.
It occurs through consistency.

A Captain's Perspective on Rewiring

When navigating strong current, fighting directly against it is a waste. Skilled captains read the water, adjust angle, and allow time for response. When planned correctly, you use them to your advantage.

Overcorrection destabilizes.
Measured correction stabilizes.

Attachment work requires the same patience.

You do not bully fear into submission.

You create conditions where fear no longer needs to dominate.

You learn to notice activation without obeying it.

You allow the body to settle before making decisions.

Internal steadiness precedes external clarity.

On a vessel, the crew can sense whether the captain is grounded or reactive.
The same is true in relationships.

Calm spreads.
So does panic.

Repatterning begins with learning to regulate your own internal storm.

What This Means for You

If you feel discouraged, consider this:

You are not resisting God.
You are not spiritually defective.
You are not failing at maturity.
You are responding from old training.

Training can be updated.

That process requires:

- Awareness
- Patience
- Safe relationships
- Honest reflection
- Repeated exposure to secure love

Rewiring rarely feels dramatic.
It feels incremental.

Small moments of staying present.
Small moments of tolerating safe discomfort.
Small moments of choosing connection without control.

A Simple Regulation Framework

When you feel activation rising:

1. Name it: "I am activated."
2. Pause breathing: Inhale slowly for four seconds, exhale for six.
3. Identify the story: "What is my fear telling me right now?"
4. Separate past from present: "Is this now — or then?"

You cannot change what you refuse to slow down long enough to observe.
Regulation begins with awareness.

The Hope

God does not rush healing.

He remains.
He repeats safety.
He anchors the heart gently until fear begins to loosen its grip.

Security grows not through force, but through faithful presence.

A seasoned captain knows that steady navigation over time carries the vessel farther than frantic over correction.

Your nervous system learned attachment through repetition.

It will relearn security the same way.

Healing is possible.

Not through striving harder.

Through attaching more securely.

In the next chapter, we will explore how secure attachment actually forms in adulthood — practically, relationally, and spiritually.

The pattern that shaped you is not your destiny.

A new course can be set.

In the end, it can hold.

CHAPTER 6

How God Heals Attachment Wounds

Attachment wounds are not healed by insight alone.

They are healed by experience.

By repeated encounters with love that is safe, steady, and present.
Love that does not disappear when fear surfaces.
Love that does not punish vulnerability.
Love that does not demand perfection to remain.

This is how God heals attachment wounds.

Not from a distance.
Through presence.

Healing Begins Where Fear Was Formed

Attachment wounds were not created by information.
They were created by experience.

Moments of distance.
Moments of unpredictability.
Moments when the nervous system concluded:

"I am not safe here."
"I am alone in this."
"I must manage this myself."

Because the wound formed through experience, healing must also come through experience.

God does not simply explain safety.

He demonstrates it.

Presence Before Performance

Many of us learned that growth comes through pressure.

Try harder.
Pray more.
Control your emotions.
Have stronger faith.

Pressure may change behavior for a season.
It does not create security.

Security forms when the heart experiences presence without pressure.

Scripture describes God as:

- compassionate
- slow to anger
- faithful
- near
- steadfast

Closeness is not the reward for healing.
It is the means of healing.

God does not wait for you to become secure before drawing near.

He draws near so that security can begin to form.

Jesus Heals by Staying

Study the way Jesus responds to fragile attachment.

Peter fails publicly.
Jesus restores him privately.

Thomas doubts openly.
Jesus invites him closer.

The disciples panic in a storm.
Jesus remains in the boat.

The Samaritan woman hides in shame.
Jesus engages her in conversation.

He does not heal by escalating.
He heals by staying.

Secure attachment is formed when love remains steady under stress.

Jesus models that repeatedly.

Trust grows not because He demands it, but because He proves Himself consistent.

Healing Is the Repetition of Safety

Attachment wounds formed through repetition.

Repeated unpredictability.
Repeated distance.
Repeated emotional absence.
Repeated lack of repair.

Healing requires repetition as well.

Repeated reassurance.
Repeated presence.
Repeated calm during conflict.
Repeated repair after rupture.

This is why Scripture emphasizes steadfast love.

Not because we fail to understand it once.
Because the nervous system needs to experience it again and again.

The first time you hear, "Nothing can separate you from My love," your mind may agree.

Your body may hesitate.

Repetition teaches the body what the mind already believes.

God Heals the Nervous System

Your nervous system was designed by God.

He does not bypass it.

When Jesus says, "Do not be afraid"— a command repeated hundreds of times throughout Scripture — He is not issuing a reprimand.
He is offering reassurance.

Healing attachment wounds is not about suppressing activation.
It is about retraining it.

That retraining happens when:

- prayer becomes a place of calm rather than striving
- Scripture becomes comfort rather than condemnation
- worship becomes grounding rather than performance
- silence becomes presence rather than abandonment

Gradually, the body begins to associate God with safety.

Breathing slows.
Shoulders soften.
Hypervigilance loosens.

Fear loses urgency when it is not reinforced.

I remember nights offshore when weather reports were unkind and the radar showed scattered cells building ahead. The first time you face that kind of unpredictability, your body stays tight. Every shift feels like threat. Every shadow or echo on the screen looks dangerous.

After years at sea, something changes. You still respect the weather. You still adjust to it. Yet your body does not spike the same way. Experience has taught you what holds and what passes.

God's presence works like that.

The first time you bring fear into prayer, your body may brace. Over time, as He remains steady, fear does not disappear instantly — but it loosens sooner. The body learns: I have weathered this before. I was not abandoned.

Vertical Security Before Horizontal Stability

Secure attachment with people becomes more sustainable when security with God deepens.

If human relationships are the only source of reassurance, they become overburdened.

God becomes the anchor.
People become companions.

"Nothing can separate us from the love of God."
— Romans 8:38–39

Many believe that verse intellectually.

Healing begins when it becomes embodied.

When silence does not equal rejection.
When delay does not equal abandonment.
When correction does not equal withdrawal.

That shift rarely happens overnight.

It unfolds through consistent experience of God remaining steady.

God Often Heals Through Safe People

Attachment wounds formed in relationship.
God often restores them in relationship.

He works through:

- trusted friends
- wise mentors
- counselors
- pastors
- small groups
- emotionally safe partners

This is not accidental.

Secure attachment is learned relationally.

When a safe person responds with:

- patience instead of distance
- curiosity instead of defensiveness
- boundaries instead of punishment
- repair instead of avoidance

the nervous system updates its map.

It learns:

"Love can stay."
"I can be honest and still be safe."
"Conflict does not mean abandonment."

That learning is powerful.

Loving Partnerships as Healing Environments

For many, romantic partnership becomes the clearest mirror of attachment wounds.

A healthy partner does not create your wounds.
But, they may activate them.

Activation is not the enemy.
Unawareness is.

When activation meets patience instead of escalation, healing begins.

When reassurance replaces dismissal, fear softens.

When boundaries replace punishment, security grows.

A loving partner cannot replace God.

They are not meant to carry the full weight of healing.

Healing flows:

From God
Through safe connection
Into the heart

A secure relationship becomes a reinforcement of vertical security, not a substitute for it.

Discernment Is Essential

Healing does not require exposure to harm.

It does not require remaining in abusive dynamics.

It does not require tolerating repeated betrayal.

God does not ask you to offer wounded places to unsafe hands.

Secure love includes boundaries.

Jesus embodied both compassion and clarity.

Healing environments are marked by safety, not chaos.

Time Is Not the Enemy

Many want attachment healing to feel dramatic.

Lightning from heaven.
Instant transformation.

God often works differently.

Trust cannot be rushed.
Security cannot be forced.

Attachment wounds formed slowly.
Healing unfolds slowly.

Slow does not mean stagnant.

Slow often means sustainable.

A Captain's Understanding of Restoration

When a vessel takes damage, the captain does not push it back into open ocean immediately.

It is docked.
Stabilized.
Inspected carefully.
Repaired with patience.
Tested in calm waters before facing heavier seas.

Internal systems are recalibrated.

Alignment is restored gradually.

God restores hearts the same way.

He does not shame damaged areas.
He tends to them.

He does not rush vessels back into storms.
He strengthens them for future weather.

Repeated exposure to steady navigation builds confidence.

Repeated exposure to steady love builds security.

What This Means for You

If healing feels slow, you are not doing it wrong.

If fear still activates, God is not disappointed.

If trust feels fragile, He has not left.

Healing often feels quiet before it feels strong.

Each time you stay present rather than retreating, a new pathway strengthens.

Each time you receive reassurance without dismissing it, safety deepens.

Each time you experience conflict without abandonment, attachment recalibrates.

Security grows gradually.

The Invitation

God's invitation is not:

"Fix yourself so I can love you."

It is:

"Let Me love you so you can heal."

As His presence becomes familiar, fear loses dominance.

As steadiness becomes predictable, hypervigilance relaxes.

As love remains consistent, attachment reorganizes.

You do not heal by striving harder.

You heal by attaching more securely.

In the next chapter, we will explore what secure attachment looks like in daily spiritual practice — how to cultivate it intentionally, patiently, and faithfully.

The sea may not always be calm.

The anchor can still hold.

The One who designed both the waters and your nervous system remains steady.

Secure love is not found in the absence of storms.

It is formed in the presence of the One who does not move.

CHAPTER 7

Healing Together: Relationships, Community, and Repair

Healing was never meant to be a solo journey.

I shared earlier from Genesis that, in the very beginning, before sin fractured trust and before fear entered the human nervous system, God made something unmistakably clear:

"It is not good for man to be alone."

Not incompetent.
Not incomplete.
Not spiritually immature.

Alone.

Isolation was never the design.

Attachment wounds were formed in relationship.
Healing unfolds there as well.

God did not design the nervous system for independence.
He designed it for connection.

God Himself exists in relationship.
Father.
Son.
Spirit.

Before humanity ever drew breath, connection existed within the Trinity.
Love was never invented at creation.
It was expressed.

Isolation is not strength.
It is distortion.

When we attempt to heal alone, we are not just resisting help.
We are resisting design.

Even Jesus, fully God and fully secure, chose disciples.
He prayed alone — but He did not live alone.
He withdrew — but He returned.

Secure people do not isolate.
They remain connected.

No Vessel Was Built to Travel the Oceans Without Support

Every seaworthy vessel has systems designed for connection.

Dock lines
Radios
Horns
Navigation channels
Crew coordination

Even the strongest ship was never meant to drift without communication or support.

I have taken vessels offshore where weather shifted faster than predicted. Weather radar lit up. Wind direction changed suddenly. Sea state built aggressively. In moments like that, responsibility rests on the captain — but survival never rests on him alone.

Crew members secure the decks.
Engineers monitor systems.
Lookouts scan the horizon.
Radios connect to other vessels.
Satellite weather updates adjust the plan.

A captain who refuses support does not prove strength.
He proves pride.

Strength does not mean isolation.
It means coordinated connection.

The human heart is no different.

You may be able to survive alone, but you were not designed to heal alone.

Why Insight Is Not Enough

You can understand your attachment style intellectually.

You can name it.
Explain it.
Diagram it.
Even teach it.

Insight is powerful.

Insight exposes patterns.

Insight does not rewire fear.

Attachment wounds are relational injuries.
They require relational repair.

Healing requires new experiences:

- Presence where abandonment once lived
- Consistency where unpredictability ruled
- Repair where rupture once remained
- Calm where intensity once dominated

These cannot be manufactured internally.

The nervous system updates through lived interaction, not self-talk alone.

The Risk of Remaining Hidden

One of the most difficult steps in healing is allowing yourself to be known.

Not performatively.
Not selectively.
Not strategically.

Actually known.

The anxious heart fears being "too much."
The avoidant heart fears being exposed.
The disorganized heart fears both closeness and rejection.

Remaining hidden feels safer.

Yet hidden wounds rarely heal.

When vulnerability meets safe presence, something shifts in the nervous system.

The body learns:

"I can be seen and still be safe."

That lesson is rarely learned in isolation.

It is learned in rooms.

In conversations.

In repair.

God Heals With Us — and Through Us

God is always the source of healing.

Yet Scripture consistently shows that He works through people.

"Carry each other's burdens, and in this way you will fulfill the law of Christ."
— Galatians 6:2

That verse assumes something profound:

You will have burdens, but you were never meant to carry them alone.

Interdependence is not weakness.

It is design.

This includes:

- Friendships that allow honesty
- Marriage rooted in mutual growth
- Healthy dating relationships anchored in God
- Mentors who offer perspective
- Counselors who create structured safety
- Faith communities that normalize imperfection

These are not replacements for God.

They are instruments in His hands.

What Healing Together Actually Looks Like

Healing together is rarely dramatic.

It looks ordinary.

It looks like:

Staying in the room during discomfort.
Returning after misunderstanding.
Admitting fault without collapsing into shame.
Not chasing when your partner needs time to regulate.
Receiving correction without retreat.
Listening without preparing a defense.

Healthy relationships are not those without conflict.

They are those with repair.

Repair is where attachment rewires.

The Power of Repair

Many attachment wounds did not form because mistakes happened.

They formed because repair never followed.

No one came back.
No one explained.
No one reassured.

Repair sounds simple:

"I see what happened."
"I see how that affected you."
"I am here."
"Let's try again."

Those words recalibrate the nervous system.

Repair tells the body:

"This is not abandonment."
"This is not rejection."
"This is not the end."

God models repair throughout Scripture.

After Israel wanders, He restores.
After Peter denies, He recommissions.
After Thomas doubts, He invites closer inspection.

Rupture does not equal rejection.

Repair builds security.

Because repair is abstract until it becomes personal.

Imagine a child who spills something and braces for anger.
Instead of yelling, a parent kneels and says,
"Let's clean this up together."

The spill becomes secondary.
Safety becomes primary.

That moment does something neurological.
It rewrites expectation.

Now imagine an adult who expresses fear in a relationship and braces for dismissal.

Instead of withdrawal, the partner says,
"I didn't realize that hurt you. I'm here."

That is repair.

Repair tells the nervous system:

"This is different than before."
"This time, you are not alone."

Repetition of repair forms security.

God's entire redemptive story is structured around repair.

Creation fractured.
God pursued.

Humanity wandered.
God restored.

Repair is not weakness.
It is covenant love in action.

The Anxious Heart Learns Stability

An anxious heart fears that one conflict equals loss.

In a secure environment, something revolutionary happens:

Conflict arises.
The relationship remains.

Distance occurs.
Connection returns.

Emotion rises.
Reassurance meets it.

The nervous system slowly updates:

"Love can survive tension."
"Closeness does not disappear because of discomfort."

That realization weakens fear's authority.

The Avoidant Heart Learns Safety in Closeness

An avoidant heart fears engulfment.

Healing begins when closeness respects autonomy.

When space is allowed without punishment.
When vulnerability is invited without force.
When needs are expressed without control.

The nervous system learns:

"I can stay connected and still remain myself."
Closeness becomes less threatening.
Distance becomes less necessary.

A Captain's Reflection on Crew Trust

Trust at sea is not built in calm conditions.

It is built when systems are tested.

I have seen green deckhands make mistakes under pressure.
Lines misjudged.
Timing off.
Communication imperfect.

The defining moment was never the mistake.

It was the response.

When correction preserved dignity, confidence grew.
When blame replaced guidance, morale fractured.

A steady captain builds steady crew.

An unpredictable captain breeds anxiety.

Leadership stability regulates the vessel.

Relational stability regulates the nervous system.

A great captain doesn't demand respect.

He earns trust through steadiness.

The Church as a Secure Base

The church was never intended to be a performance hall.

It was designed to be a secure base.

A place where:

Imperfection is acknowledged.
Growth is gradual.
Grace is practiced.
Presence outweighs performance.

When churches shame vulnerability, attachment wounds deepen.

When churches model secure love, healing accelerates.

Community reflects God's character when it remains steady under stress.

What Healing Together Is Not

Healing together does not mean:

Oversharing without discernment.
Ignoring red flags.
Remaining in unsafe environments.
Forcing vulnerability.
Abandoning boundaries.

Secure love includes clarity.

God never calls you to expose wounds to unsafe hands.

Discernment protects growth.

Learning to Stay

One of the strongest signs of attachment growth is learning how to stay.

Stay present when discomfort rises.
Stay engaged when fear whispers escape.
Stay open when shame urges hiding.

Staying does not mean tolerating harm.

It means tolerating growth.

God stays with you.

Over time, you learn to stay with others.

Staying is one of the rarest forms of strength.

Staying when your chest tightens.
Staying when silence feels loud.
Staying when shame whispers, "Leave before they see you."

Early attachment often trained you to escape discomfort.

Healing trains you to regulate inside it.

I have navigated narrow inlets where turning around would have been easier than staying the course. Current pushed sideways. Wind shifted unpredictably. The temptation was to power out and retreat.

Sometimes the safest option is not escape.
It is steady correction.

Staying does not mean enduring harm.
It means not abandoning growth.

Over time, the nervous system learns:

"Discomfort is not destruction."
"Conflict is not catastrophe."
"Repair is possible."

That is how secure attachment forms in real time.

A Secure Pattern Emerges

As healing continues, change becomes visible.

You begin to:

Pause before reacting.
Ask before assuming.
Communicate instead of withdrawing.

Receive love without suspicion.
Trust that repair is possible.

Security is quiet.

It shows up in steady responses.
In measured tone.
In consistent presence.

Anchored Together

Healing with God and with others does not create dependence.

It creates security.

Security is not standing alone.

It is knowing you are held.

Held by God.
Supported by community.
Strengthened through repair.

No vessel was meant to drift indefinitely.

Anchors exist for a reason.

Safe people also exist for a reason.

The Invitation

If you have been trying to heal alone, consider this:

Isolation may feel safer.
It does not lead to wholeness.

Invite safe people in.
Choose environments marked by steadiness.
Allow yourself to be known gradually.

Let repair teach your nervous system what abandonment never could.

God holds you securely.

He often places others around you so that security becomes tangible.

Be careful not to turn away from the resources He places before you.

Healing together is not weakness.

It is design.

When the sea rises,
navigation is steadier
when you are not steering alone.

CHAPTER 8

Breaking Generational Cycles: Becoming the Safe One

Healing does not stop with you.

That may feel heavy at first.
It is not meant to feel heavy.
It is meant to feel hopeful.

Pain travels through generations.

So does healing.

Many of us grew up in homes where love existed — but safety did not.
Provision was present — but emotional connection was inconsistent.
Faith was taught — but vulnerability was uncomfortable.
Discipline was clear — but repair was rare or nonexistent.

Without realizing it, we absorbed patterns.

Not because our parents were evil.
Not because they did not care.
Because they were shaped by what shaped them.

Generational cycles sometimes begin with cruelty.
More often, they begin with unhealed wounds.

What remains unexamined becomes repeated.
What remains unhealed becomes inherited.
What remains unnamed quietly becomes identity.

Attachment Is Passed Down Through Experience

Children do not learn attachment from lectures.
They learn it from experience.

They learn from:

- How caregivers respond to tears
- How anger is expressed
- How affection is offered or withheld
- How conflict is handled
- How quickly, if at all, repair follows rupture
- Whether it feels safe to bring big emotions into the room

Attachment is absorbed.
It is caught long before it is understood.

A child does not analyze a parent's nervous system.
A child internalizes it.

If the home is tense, the body learns vigilance.
If the home is distant, the body learns self-reliance.
If the home is unpredictable, the body learns scanning.
If the home is secure, the body learns calm.

No one has to explain the pattern.
The nervous system encodes it.

Generational cycles are not only behavioral.
They are neurological.

Which means when you heal your nervous system,
you interrupt a lineage.

You alter inheritance at its source.

A Story of Control… and a Different Outcome

Christy grew up in a house where control meant safety.

Her mother managed everything.
Schedules.

Tone.
Appearances.
Emotions.

Nothing chaotic was allowed to remain visible for long.

If Christy cried too loudly, she was told to compose herself.
If she was angry, she was corrected for disrespect.
If she disagreed, she was reminded who was in charge.

The house ran efficiently.

It did not run safely.

Christy learned something quietly:

Strong emotion creates instability.
Instability must be contained.
Containment requires control.

Years later, Christy became a mother.

Her daughter, Emma, was fiery.
Curious.
Sensitive.
Intense.

One afternoon, Emma collapsed on the floor in frustration over a broken toy.

The crying was loud.
The emotion messy.

Christy felt her body tighten.

Her jaw locked.
Her shoulders rose.
Her voice wanted to sharpen.

"Enough. Get up. That's ridiculous."

The familiar impulse to shut it down moved quickly through her.

Control the noise.
Control the emotion.
Control the room.

But something new interrupted the pattern.

Not perfection.

Awareness.

Christy recognized the surge in her own nervous system.

She wasn't angry at Emma.

She was afraid of chaos.

For the first time in her life, she chose something different.

Instead of silencing the emotion, she moved toward it.

She sat beside her daughter on the floor.

"That's really disappointing, isn't it?" she said gently.

Emma nodded through tears.

They stayed there together.

The toy was still broken.
The emotion was no longer alone.

In that moment, Christy did not just comfort her child.

She dismantled a generational equation:

Emotion does not equal loss of control.
Intensity does not equal instability.
Connection does not require suppression.

Emma's nervous system learned safety.

Christy's nervous system learned something new as well.

Control was no longer the only path to calm.

That is how generational cycles shift.

Not through force.

Through attunement.

The Turning Point Is Awareness

For generations, patterns can move forward quietly.

Anger passed as discipline.
Silence passed as strength.
Overcontrol passed as protection.
Emotional distance passed as maturity.

Until someone notices.
Until someone pauses.
Until someone asks:

"Why do I react this way?"
"Why does this feel so intense?"
"Why does closeness feel threatening?"

Awareness is not blame.
It is interruption.
It is the moment the wheel turns.

Scripture calls this renewal.

"Be transformed by the renewing of your mind."
— Romans 12:2

Renewal does not only change belief.
It changes response.
It changes tone.
It changes regulation.
It changes legacy.

Becoming the Safe One

To become the safe one does not mean becoming perfect.

It means becoming aware enough to choose differently.

Aware of:

- Your triggers
- Your tone shifts
- Your withdrawal tendencies
- Your pursuit patterns
- Your fear of abandonment
- Your fear of engulfment

Awareness creates space.

In that space, choice becomes possible.

Instead of reacting automatically, you pause.
Instead of escalating, you regulate.
Instead of withdrawing, you communicate.
Instead of blaming, you repair.

These moments feel small.

They are not.

They are generational pivots.

Predictable Love Changes Everything

One of the most powerful healing forces in the world is predictable love.

Predictable love does not disappear under stress.
It does not shame emotion.
It does not weaponize vulnerability.
It does not withdraw to regain control.
It does not escalate to prove authority.

Predictable love says:

"I am here."
"We can work through this."
"You are safe with me."

Children who grow up with predictable love do not have to brace for connection.
Spouses who experience predictable love do not have to scan for threat.
Crews who experience predictable leadership do not flinch under correction.

When you heal, you become predictable.

Not rigid.
Not emotionless.

Steady.

That steadiness becomes a refuge for others.

A Story of Partnership and Repair

Elena grew up with emotional chaos.

Her mother was affectionate one day and withdrawn the next.
Conflict meant slammed doors.
Silence meant danger.

As an adult, Elena married Daniel — steady, calm, reserved.

The first time Daniel asked for space after an argument, her body panicked.

"He's leaving," her nervous system whispered.
"It's starting again."

She pursued.
He retreated.
She escalated.
He shut down.

The old dance began.

One evening, after a tense exchange, Daniel did something neither of them had experienced growing up.

He came back.

Not to defend.
Not to correct.

To repair.

"I'm not going anywhere," he said quietly.
"I just needed a minute to calm down. I'm still here."

Her body did not trust him immediately.

Years of wiring do not dissolve in a sentence.

But something shifted.

The next time conflict surfaced, he returned again.
And again.
And again.

Consistency retrained expectation.

Elena began to realize:

Space did not equal abandonment.
Conflict did not equal collapse.
Repair was possible.

That is how secure partnership becomes generational healing.

Not by avoiding conflict.
By practicing repair.

Remember, your children don't just see how you react them — they also see how you react to others.

What Children Learn From Watching Your Relationships

Children are always studying the emotional climate of the home.

Not consciously.

Nervously.

They are watching:

How you speak to your spouse when you are frustrated.
How you handle disagreement.
Whether sarcasm replaces honesty.
Whether silence replaces repair.
Whether affection returns after tension.
Whether you run when conflict arises.

They are learning what adult love looks like long before they ever experience it themselves.

A child does not need to sit in the middle of an argument to be shaped by it.

They hear tone through walls.
They feel distance across dinner tables.
They notice when one parent withdraws and the other pursues.
They sense when apologies never come.
They feel it deeply when you walk away instead of repairing.

They also notice when repair does happen.

When a father circles back and says,
"I was short earlier. I'm sorry."

When a mother softens her tone and says,
"That came out wrong. Let's try that again."

When two adults disagree — and remain connected.

Those moments teach something profound:

Conflict is survivable.
Love does not evaporate under pressure.

Voices can lower.
People can return.

Children internalize not only how you respond to them, but how you respond to each other.

If love looks unpredictable, they will brace for unpredictability.
If love looks distant, they will prepare for distance.
If love looks volatile, they will scan for volatility.
If love looks steady — even when imperfect — they will learn steadiness.

A home where parents repair becomes a training ground for secure attachment.

A home where tension is ignored becomes a training ground for avoidance.

A home where anger dominates becomes a training ground for hypervigilance.

Your partnership is not separate from your parenting.

It is part of it.

Even if you are divorced.
Even if you are co-parenting.
Even if you are dating.

Children are learning what connection means by watching how you navigate it.

They are learning:

How to speak.
How to apologize.
How to handle emotion.
How to stay.

How to leave.
How to return.

You are modeling their future nervous system in real time.

That may sound intimidating.

It is not meant to create pressure.
It is meant to create intention.

You do not need to eliminate conflict.
You need to demonstrate repair.
You do not need to hide tension.
You need to show what healthy reconciliation looks like.

When children see two adults move through disagreement without humiliation, abandonment, or fear, something stabilizes inside them.

They learn:

Love can be strong without being loud.
Boundaries can exist without cruelty.
Space can exist without rejection.
Repair can follow rupture.

That lesson will travel with them into every future relationship.

Parenting Through a Secure Lens

Parents carry immense influence — not because they are perfect, but because they are primary regulators.

Children need structure.
They need boundaries.
They need guidance.

They also need attunement.

They need to know:

"My emotions are not too much."
"My caregiver can handle my distress."
"I am loved even when I fail."
"Repair will come."

No parent achieves this flawlessly.

Secure attachment is not built through perfection.
It is built through repair.

When a parent says:

"I was too harsh."
"I'm sorry."
"I love you."

A child's nervous system updates.

Mistake does not equal rejection.
Conflict does not equal loss of love.
Failure does not equal abandonment.

That is how cycles shift.

Breaking Cycles Without Blame

Generational healing does not require hostility toward the past.

Many caregivers did the best they could with limited tools.
They loved deeply.
They simply lacked regulation, insight, or support.

Understanding does not excuse harm.
It allows compassion to coexist with responsibility.

Blame keeps you emotionally fused to the past.
Compassion allows differentiation.

You can honor what was good while choosing to improve what was unstable.

That is maturity.

A Captain's Reflection on Wake

Every vessel leaves a wake.

Some wakes are violent — churning water that destabilizes smaller boats long after the ship has passed.

Other wakes are steady — manageable, predictable, easy to navigate.

When I steer through a channel, I pay attention not only to what is ahead, but to what is going on behind me as well.

Speed affects wake.
Correction affects wake.
Awareness affects wake.

Careless captains focus only on forward progress.
Seasoned captains consider impact.

Your life leaves a wake.

The way you respond under stress.
The way you correct mistakes.
The way you handle emotion.
The way you repair rupture.

Children learn from that wake.
Spouses adapt to that wake.
Communities regulate around that wake.

Healing changes the wake you leave.

Calmer wakes are easier to follow.

Leadership and Generational Culture

This applies beyond family.

Unhealed leaders pass down anxiety.
Reactive leaders create reactive environments.
Avoidant leaders create emotionally distant cultures.
Disorganized leaders create confusion.

Secure leaders create steadiness.

When leaders regulate first, others settle.
When leaders repair publicly, trust deepens.
When leaders tolerate vulnerability, safety spreads.

Culture is attachment scaled.

Which means your healing impacts more than your household.

God's Patience Across Generations

Scripture reveals a God who works beyond one lifetime.

"The Lord is compassionate and gracious, slow to anger, abounding in love."
— Psalm 103:8

God is not intimidated by entrenched patterns.
He is not discouraged by family history.
He is not limited by what you inherited.

He restores what was fractured.
He steadies what was unstable.
He repairs what was ignored.

Generational healing is not dramatic.

It is faithful.

Becoming the Turning Point

Every generational cycle has a turning point.

Someone who pauses.
Someone who seeks help.
Someone who repairs.
Someone who regulates.
Someone who refuses to escalate inherited fear.

That someone may be you.

Breaking cycles is rarely loud.
It is incremental.
Quiet.
Repetitive.

Until one day you notice:

Your child does not brace the way you did.
Your spouse does not fear the way you once feared.
Your crew does not flinch under correction.
Your church feels safe to confess weakness.

That is generational transformation.

The Invitation

You cannot rewrite what shaped you.
You can reshape what follows you.

You cannot undo inherited instability.
You can become steady.

Become the safe one.
Become the one who repairs.
The one who regulates.
The one whose tone lowers instead of rises.
The one who stays when tension builds.

Not because you are flawless.

Because you are healing.

God does not merely restore individuals.

He restores legacies.

When traveling the sea, the wake you leave
will either multiply chaos or model steadiness.

Choose steadiness.

Not for image.
Not for applause.
Not for perfection.

For those coming behind you.

It will travel farther than you will ever see.

CHAPTER 9

When Love Is Tested: Triggers, Conflict, and Growth

If healing were linear, most of us would already be finished.

It is not.

Healing does not move in straight lines.
It moves in spirals.
Forward.
Backward.
Sideways.
Deeper.

Often revisiting familiar emotional terrain — but from a different level of awareness.

Nothing exposes attachment patterns faster than intimacy.

The closer the relationship, the louder the triggers.

The more important the bond, the greater the activation.

Intensity is not a flaw in love.
It is evidence that love matters.

Why the Closest Relationships Trigger the Most

Triggers rarely show up with strangers.

They show up with the person you trust.
The person you need.
The person whose presence regulates your nervous system.

A partner's silence.
A delayed response.
A shift in tone.
A request for space.
A boundary that feels unfamiliar.

To one nervous system, it is neutral.
To another, it is threat.

The closer the bond, the more vulnerable the attachment system becomes.

A coworker's irritation may sting.

A spouse's withdrawal can feel catastrophic.

This is not because you are weak.

It is because attachment amplifies significance.

Significance amplifies fear.

The Paradox of Deep Love

The deeper the attachment, the greater the risk.

Not because love is unsafe.
Because love matters.

Ethan had never felt safer than he did with Naomi.
That was the problem.

With past relationships, distance was familiar.
He knew how to operate there.

With Naomi, he felt seen.

One evening, during a simple disagreement about finances, she said, "I just need to know you're in this with me."

Her words were steady.

His body reacted as if accused.

In childhood, being questioned meant being inadequate.
Inadequacy meant shame.
Shame meant withdrawal.

His chest tightened.
His tone sharpened.

"Why are you making this a big deal?"

She wasn't.
His history was.

Later that night, alone, he realized something unsettling.

The safer he felt with her, the more terrifying it was to disappoint her.

The more he loved her, the more activated he became when he thought he might lose her.

Deep attachment increases emotional volume.

The relationship you care about most will often expose the wound you've protected longest.

That is not dysfunction.

That is significance.

Significance demands growth.

What Triggers Really Are

A trigger is not weakness.

It is stored memory.

It is the nervous system reacting before logic can intervene.

Triggers are moments when the present brushes against the past.

They often appear as:

- Sudden panic
- Emotional flooding
- Shutdown
- Urgent pursuit
- Withdrawal
- Anger that feels disproportionate
- Defensiveness that feels automatic

When the reaction feels larger than the moment,
history is involved.

The body is not only responding to now.
It is responding to then.

A Story of Escalation

Mark valued independence.
Claire valued closeness.

They loved deeply.
They also activated deeply.

One evening, after a long day, Mark came home quiet.
He was mentally exhausted.

Claire felt the shift immediately.

"Are you okay?" she asked.

"I'm fine," he replied, short but not harsh.

Her nervous system tightened.

Fine meant distance in her childhood home.
Fine meant something was wrong but not being said.

She leaned in harder.

"Did I do something?"

"No," he sighed.

The sigh felt like confirmation.

Her tone sharpened.

His shoulders stiffened.

Within minutes, they were arguing about tone, not exhaustion.

Neither of them intended harm.

Both were protecting something older.

Claire was protecting against emotional abandonment.
Mark was protecting against emotional overwhelm.

The turning point did not come when they stopped fighting.

It came when they slowed down.

Later that night, Claire said quietly,

"When you go quiet, my body feels like I'm about to lose you."

Mark paused.

"When things escalate, my body feels like I'm failing you."

Neither statement accused.

Both revealed.

That conversation did not eliminate future triggers.

It reduced distortion.

That is growth.

When Space Activates Fear

Few experiences activate attachment more intensely than distance.

Temporary breakups.
Requests for space.
Cooling-off periods.
Emotional separation without clear resolution.

Distance can feel like danger.

Even when it is meant to create clarity.

Cognitive Dissonance in Separation

Cognitive dissonance occurs when two opposing truths exist at the same time.

"I love this person."
"This hurts."

"They say they care."
"They are pulling away."

"We are good together."
"This feels unstable."

The mind seeks relief from contradiction.

When clarity is unavailable, distortion often fills the gap.

Distance without regulation magnifies distortion.

A Story of Space and Distortion

Lena and Aaron had built something meaningful.

Not perfect.
Not effortless.
But real.

After a series of intense arguments, they agreed to take two weeks apart.

Not to end things.
To breathe.

The first few days were quiet.

By day five, Lena's nervous system was loud.

He hasn't called.
He doesn't miss me.
Maybe he's relieved.
Maybe I was the problem.

Memories began rearranging themselves.

Moments of affection felt smaller.
Moments of tension felt larger.

Cognitive dissonance began rewriting the narrative.

Aaron was having his own spiral.

Maybe we aren't compatible.
Maybe love shouldn't feel this hard.
Maybe she deserves someone more emotionally available.

Both still loved each other.

Both were flooded.

Space amplified interpretation.

Neither of them was seeing clearly.

The breakthrough did not happen during distance.

It happened when they reconnected.

Instead of defending conclusions formed in isolation, they shared fears.

Lena admitted, "When you didn't reach out, my mind told me I never mattered."

Aaron admitted, "When things escalated, my mind told me I was incapable of giving you what you needed."

Neither of those statements reflected reality.

They reflected fear.

Naming fear reduced distortion.

Distortion had been louder than truth.

That is what cognitive dissonance does when attachment is activated.

It muddies the waters.

Regulation clears them.

Conflict Is Not the Enemy

Healthy relationships are not conflict-free.

They are repair-rich.

Avoidance erodes intimacy faster than disagreement ever could.

Secure conflict includes:

- Staying present
- Speaking honestly without attacking
- Listening without preparing defense
- Taking breaks without disappearing
- Returning after overwhelm
- Repairing consistently

Healing does not eliminate tension.

It makes tension survivable.

When Growth Feels Like Regression

Sometimes healing feels worse before it feels better.

You may feel triggers more intensely.

You may think:

"I thought I was past this."

You are not regressing.

You are noticing.

Awareness precedes mastery.

You cannot regulate what you refuse to acknowledge.

A Captain's Perspective on Surviving Storms

Calm water proves nothing.

Storms reveal everything.

Loose fittings surface.
Crew coordination becomes visible.
Structural weaknesses announce themselves.

The goal is not to eliminate weather.

It is to build vessels capable of navigating it.

Relationships are no different.

Pressure does not create weakness.

It exposes it.

Exposure allows reinforcement.

Reinforcement builds endurance.

The Sacred Pause

Between trigger and reaction lies a sacred space.

The pause.

The pause sounds like:

"I'm overwhelmed."

"This is touching something old."

"I want to stay connected, but I need to slow down."

The pause interrupts generational reflex.

It protects attachment from distortion.

God's Steadiness in Activation

God is not intimidated by your triggers.

He does not withdraw when emotions rise.

He does not shame your reactions.

Once again:

"The Lord is compassionate and gracious,
slow to anger, abounding in love."
— Psalm 103:8

His steadiness models what secure love looks like.

Over time, His consistency retrains your response.

When Love Is Truly Tested

Love is not tested in ease.

It is tested in misunderstanding.

In temporary distance.

In moments when cognitive dissonance whispers extremes.

In the space between fear and repair.

The strongest relationships are not those without activation.

They are those where activation leads to awareness.

Awareness leads to communication.

Communication leads to repair.

Repair leads to security.

The Invitation

If you are in a season where love feels tested:

Where triggers are loud.
Where space feels confusing.
Where conflict feels heavier than expected.
Where your mind is telling stories you are not sure are true.

You are not failing.

You are in the work.

Healing does not mean avoiding storms.

It means learning how to navigate them
without abandoning the vessel.

Security is not the absence of intensity.

It is the ability to remain steady inside it.

That steadiness is built one regulated moment at a time.

CHAPTER 10

Living Securely: Boundaries, Trust, and Rest

Living securely doesn't mean living without fear.
It means fear no longer gets the final word.

Secure attachment is not a personality trait you are born with or without.
It is a relational posture that forms when safety becomes familiar and love becomes predictable.

As healing deepens, something subtle begins to shift.
You stop living from survival.
You begin living from stability.

You still feel emotion.
You still experience disappointment.
You still get triggered at times.

But you recover faster.
You regulate sooner.
You return more easily.

You start to live from a different place.
Not reactive.
Rooted.

Rooted people still sway.
They just don't uproot.

What Secure Living Actually Feels Like

Secure living does not feel dramatic.
It feels steady.

It looks like:
• responding instead of reacting
• expressing needs without apologizing for them
• tolerating closeness without panic
• tolerating distance without despair

• trusting repair is possible
• resting instead of bracing

Secure people still feel hurt.
They just do not assume hurt equals abandonment.

They still feel fear.
They just do not let fear steer.

They do not scan every silence for rejection.
They do not interpret every disagreement as collapse.
They do not interpret every boundary as betrayal.

Their nervous system has learned something new:

"I can survive this."
"Connection can stretch without breaking."
"I am still safe."

That is secure living.
It is quiet strength.
It is emotional endurance.
It is regulated presence.

A Story of Quiet Strength

Mike had spent most of his adult life chasing reassurance.
If his partner seemed distant, he pursued.
If texts went unanswered, he spiraled.
If conflict arose, he escalated to regain closeness.

After years of therapy and intentional growth, something began to change.

One evening, his wife said,
"I need some space tonight. I'm overwhelmed."

The old version of Mike would have heard:

"I'm tired of you."
"You are too much."
"This is the beginning of the end."

But this time, he paused.

He felt the activation.
The tightening in his chest.
The familiar urge to argue for connection.

Instead of reacting, he breathed.

"Okay," he said gently. "I'm here when you're ready."

He went for a walk.
Not to withdraw.
To regulate.

The relationship did not collapse.
She returned.
They reconnected.

The difference was not that fear disappeared.
The difference was that fear did not dictate behavior.

That is secure growth.
Not the absence of activation.
The presence of choice.

A Story of Calm Under Pressure

Edward had always believed intensity meant passion. Raised in a loud household where emotion equaled volume, he associated calm with disinterest.

When his fiancée, Rachel, stayed composed during disagreement, he felt uneasy.

"Why aren't you reacting?" he once asked.

"I am reacting," she replied softly. "I just don't need to raise my voice to be heard."

It unsettled him.
He mistook steadiness for detachment.
He mistook regulation for emotional distance.

Over time, he realized something profound:

Her calm was not withdrawal.
It was capacity.

She could stay present without escalating.
She could disagree without destabilizing.

He began to learn a new equation:

Stability is not indifference.
It is strength.

That shift changed how he defined love.

Boundaries Are a Sign of Security, Not Distance

One of the most misunderstood aspects of secure attachment is boundaries.
Insecure attachment confuses boundaries with rejection.
Secure attachment understands boundaries as clarity.

Boundaries are not walls.
They are defined edges that protect connection.

Without boundaries:

- resentment builds
- exhaustion increases
- emotional enmeshment forms
- identity blurs

With boundaries:

- connection remains sustainable
- individuality stays intact
- respect deepens

Jesus modeled this consistently.
He loved deeply.
He served generously.
He withdrew to rest.
He said no.
He did not heal every person.
He did not respond to every demand.

Secure love is not overextended love.
It is sustainable love.

Boundaries say:

"I can love you without losing myself."
"I can stay connected without being consumed."
"I can disappoint you and still care."

That balance is maturity.

When Boundaries Trigger Others

When you begin living securely, not everyone will feel comfortable.
People accustomed to your over-accommodation may interpret boundaries as distance.

People accustomed to your emotional pursuit may interpret steadiness as detachment.

Growth shifts relational dynamics.
That does not mean growth is wrong.
It means the system is recalibrating.

Secure living may temporarily unsettle insecure patterns around you.
Stay steady.
Over time, consistency clarifies intention.

Trust Grows Where Consistency Lives

Trust is not built through promises.
It is built through repetition.

Secure attachment forms when love shows up consistently — especially when it would be easier not to.

Trust grows when:

- someone returns after conflict
- someone follows through repeatedly
- someone remains calm under stress
- someone tells the truth even when uncomfortable

This applies horizontally.
It also applies vertically.

Many struggle to trust God not because He is inconsistent, but because early attachment trained them to expect inconsistency.

Over time, repeated experiences of God's steadiness retrain expectation.

You begin to internalize:

"He did not leave."
"He did not shame."
"He did not disappear."

Trust becomes embodied.
Not forced.

Learning to Rest Without Guilt

One of the clearest signs of healing is the ability to rest.
Anxious attachment struggles to rest because rest feels like abandonment.
Avoidant attachment struggles to rest because rest feels unproductive.
Disorganized attachment struggles to rest because rest feels unfamiliar.
Secure attachment rests because it trusts.

Scripture says:

"Come to Me, all who are weary and burdened, and I will give you rest."
— Matthew 11:28

Rest is not laziness.
It is regulation.
It is nervous system permission.
It is the internal belief:

"I do not have to earn safety."

A Captain's Understanding of Rest

At sea, a steady rhythm determines survival.
You cannot run engines at full throttle indefinitely.
You cannot ignore maintenance.
You cannot push crew beyond capacity without consequence.

Fatigue creates error.
Error creates danger.

Experienced captains know:

Rest is not optional.
It is strategic.

Weather offshore does not care how tired you are.
Navigation errors multiply under exhaustion.

Secure leadership requires regulated leadership.
Secure living requires the same.

If you live in constant emotional full throttle, you will misread relational cues.

Rest recalibrates perception.
Rest prevents unnecessary escalation.
Rest protects the vessel.

Living Securely Is a Practice, Not a Destination

Security is not a finish line.
It is a rhythm.

Some days you will respond beautifully.
Other days old patterns will tug.

That does not erase progress.
It reveals integration still underway.

Living securely means returning — again and again — to what is true:
"I am safe."
"I can regulate."
"I can repair."
"I can stay."

Security is built in repetition.

Vertical Security: God as the Anchor

As attachment heals, something shifts spiritually.
Prayer becomes less frantic.
Silence becomes less threatening.
Scripture feels less condemning.
God's presence feels less distant.

You stop asking, "Are You here?"

You begin trusting, "You are here."

Secure attachment vertically does not eliminate doubt.
It eliminates panic.

God becomes the anchor — not the emergency rescue.
Anchors do not prevent storms.
They prevent drifting.

You begin living anchored.
Not drifting.

When Fear No Longer Steers

Living securely does not mean fear vanishes.
It means fear does not captain the ship.

Fear may still speak.
It simply does not command.

Security means:

You feel activation — and pause.
You feel distance — and breathe.
You feel conflict — and stay.

You choose alignment over impulse.
That is maturity.
That is integration.

The Invitation

Living securely does not mean perfection.
It means alignment.

It means your nervous system, your faith, your relationships, and your identity are increasingly synchronized.

You are no longer living in reaction to what happened.
You are living from what is true.

Fear may still visit.
Again, it no longer drives the ship.
God does.

As you continue healing, you will notice something remarkable:

You rest more.
You pursue less.
You trust deeper.
You love freer.

Not because you tried harder.
Because your heart finally believes it is safe.

When the sea rises,
you no longer grip the wheel in panic.
You steady it.
You adjust.
You breathe.
You continue forward.

CHAPTER 11

When Healing Leads to Reconciliation — and When Wisdom Must Lead the Way

One of the quiet fears many people carry as they begin healing is this:

If I grow, will I lose the people I love?

If I become healthier, will this relationship have to end?

For some, healing feels like a threat to connection rather than a pathway toward it.

Let's say this clearly from the beginning:

Healing does not mean giving up on relationships.

In fact, healing often makes reconciliation possible for the first time.

Growth does not automatically require separation.

Sometimes growth is the very thing that makes restoration possible.

Healing Is Not a Call to Abandonment

We live in a culture that is quick to discard.

Quick to label.
Quick to diagnose.
Quick to walk away.
Quick to say, "This is just who I am."
Quick to say, "You deserve better."
Quick to assume incompatibility where there may simply be unhealed wounds.

But God is not a God of disposability.

He is a God of restoration.

Scripture tells us:

"God was reconciling the world to Himself in Christ."
— 2 Corinthians 5:19

Reconciliation is not a side note in the Gospel.

It is central.

So, it matters that we say this carefully but confidently:

Most relationships are not broken beyond repair.

They are strained because two wounded people are operating from unhealed places.

Attachment wounds create distortion.

Distortion creates misunderstanding.
Misunderstanding creates defensiveness.
Defensiveness creates distance.

That distance eventually begins to feel like incompatibility.

But often, what we are experiencing is not incompatibility.

It is untreated fear.

A Story of Misinterpreted Distance

Steve and Hannah loved each other deeply.

But love alone did not prevent friction.

Steve valued space when overwhelmed.
Hannah valued closeness when stressed.

When conflict arose, Steve would go quiet.

Hannah would lean in harder.

He felt crowded.
She felt abandoned.

He withdrew further.
She escalated further.

Eventually both reached the same painful conclusion:

"This may not work."

What they did not yet understand was attachment.

Steve's withdrawal was not lack of love.

It was emotional regulation learned in childhood.

Hannah's pursuit was not control.

It was fear of emotional disappearance.

Once they began understanding their patterns, their language shifted.

Instead of saying:

"You don't care."

"You're suffocating me."

They began saying:

"When you go quiet, I feel alone."

"When things escalate, I feel overwhelmed."

Understanding did not eliminate conflict overnight.

But it replaced accusation with insight.

That shift made reconciliation possible.

Cognitive Dissonance in Seasons of Separation

Few experiences activate the attachment system more intensely than separation.

Not permanent endings.

Temporary distance.

A break.
A cooling-off period.
A season of space.
A pause to seek clarity.

Separation is not neutral to the nervous system.

It feels like threat.

When threat meets uncertainty, cognitive dissonance often follows.

A reminder from Chapter 9:

Cognitive dissonance occurs when two opposing realities exist at the same time:

"I love this person."
"This hurts."

"They say they care."
"They are pulling away."

"We are good together."
"This feels unstable."

The brain does not tolerate contradiction easily.

So, it resolves tension by rewriting narrative.

Memories rearrange.
Positive moments shrink.
Negative moments enlarge.

Certainty replaces nuance.

The anxious heart may conclude:
"I never mattered."

The avoidant heart may conclude:
"We were never compatible."

Neither conclusion necessarily reflects truth.

They reflect fear seeking relief.

Separation without regulation becomes **story-building**.

Separation with maturity becomes **clarity-building**.

The difference determines whether distance destroys a relationship or refines it.

When Cognitive Dissonance Finally Breaks

Cognitive dissonance rarely lasts forever.

Over time, truth tends to surface.

As emotional activation settles and perspective returns, many people begin to see their relationship more clearly.

Memories rebalance.

Nuance returns.

The story becomes less extreme.

Sometimes people realize:

"We were not enemies."
"We were two wounded people reacting from fear."

But there is an important reality that must be acknowledged.

Sometimes this clarity arrives **after the window for reconciliation has closed**.

A partner may have moved forward.
A relationship may have permanently shifted.
Life may have taken both people down different paths.

This is one of the quiet and heavy tragedies of unresolved cognitive dissonance.

When fear rewrites the story too quickly, decisions may follow before clarity arrives.

That is why emotional regulation during seasons of separation matters so deeply.

Because clarity reached early enough can preserve the possibility of repair.

Clarity reached too late may simply explain what was lost.

This can be one of the most tragic things to happen in our deepest and most loving relationships.

A Story of Separation and Return

James and Olivia agreed to take thirty days apart.

Not to end things.
To breathe.

Their arguments had intensified.
Communication had collapsed into reactivity.

Both loved each other.

Neither felt safe.

Week one felt calm.

Week two felt loud.

James began replaying every argument.
Every sharp word.
Every moment he felt inadequate.

His mind whispered:

"This shouldn't be this hard."

Olivia began replaying every silence.
Every time she felt unseen.
Every moment she felt alone.

Her mind whispered:

"He was never fully here."

Cognitive dissonance was rewriting both of their stories.

Pain was reshaping memory.

But something different happened in week three.

Instead of building a case, they sought counsel.

Instead of rehearsing conclusions, they journaled their triggers.

Instead of asking, "Were we wrong for each other?" they began asking, "What was being activated in us?"

When they met again, the tone was different.

James said, "When conflict rose, I shut down because I felt incapable."

Olivia said, "When you shut down, I panicked because I felt abandoned."

The separation had not destroyed love.

It had exposed distortion.

Reconciliation did not happen because distance felt good.

It happened because both people did the work while apart.

Separation became preparation.

Journaling Your Triggers

One of the most powerful tools for understanding attachment activation is simple:

Write it down.

When emotions rise, the nervous system moves quickly.

Thoughts blur together.
Feelings intensify.
Stories form before awareness catches up.

Journaling slows the process.

Instead of reacting outwardly, you begin observing inwardly.

When you notice strong emotional activation, try three simple steps.

1. **Notice**

Pay attention to the moment your body reacts.

Is your chest tightening?
Is your breathing shallow?
Are you suddenly angry, anxious, or shut down?

Activation begins in the body before it reaches the mind.

2. **Name**

Write down what you believe you are feeling.

"I feel abandoned."
"I feel overwhelmed."
"I feel unimportant."
"I feel criticized."

Naming the emotion begins separating the present moment from past experiences.

3. **Sort**

Ask yourself two questions:

"What just happened?"
"What does this remind me of?"

Many triggers are not about the present moment alone.

They are echoes of earlier experiences.

Sorting these reactions allows you to see the difference between what is happening now and what your nervous system remembers from before.

Over time, journaling creates awareness.

Awareness creates space between **trigger** and **reaction**.

That space is where healing begins.

Reconciliation Requires Work on Both Sides

Here is a truth that must be held gently but firmly:

Reconciliation is possible when both people are willing to grow.

Not when one person does all the work.

Not when one person carries all the insight.

Not when one person heals while the other refuses reflection.

True reconciliation requires of **both** parties:

- humility
- accountability
- willingness to learn
- willingness to repair
- willingness to tolerate discomfort
- commitment to growth

Scripture reminds us:

"As far as it depends on you, live at peace with everyone."
— Romans 12:18

Peace is pursued.

It is not forced.

You can offer repair.

You cannot manufacture reciprocity.

The Five Conditions of Healthy Reconciliation

When reconciliation becomes possible, certain conditions almost always appear.

1. **Ownership without defensiveness**
   Both individuals acknowledge their contributions to the fracture.
2. **Regulation during conflict**
   Disagreements remain possible, but escalation decreases.
3. **Repeated repair**
   Apologies become normal rather than rare.
4. **Behavioral consistency**
   Words and actions align over time.
5. **Shared commitment to growth**
   Both people pursue healing rather than defending their patterns.

Without these conditions, reconciliation remains fragile.

With them, reconciliation becomes transformation.

A Reconciliation Manifesto

Let this be said clearly:

Most relationships are not beyond redemption.

They are buried under:

- unregulated nervous systems
- misinterpreted behavior
- untreated trauma
- pride
- shame
- fear
- lack of language

We must stop confusing activation with incompatibility.
We must stop labeling struggle as disqualification.
We must stop discarding people for symptoms that can be healed.

Mental illness does not disqualify someone from love.

Attachment insecurity does not disqualify someone from commitment.

Trauma does not make someone disposable.

Struggle is human.

Refusal is destructive.

Secure love can endure struggle.

It cannot survive chronic unwillingness.

Reconciliation is not naïve optimism.

It is disciplined hope.

But Healing Also Brings Clarity

Healing does not mean enduring abuse.

It does not mean tolerating harm.

It does not mean staying where accountability is refused.

It does not mean accepting chronic betrayal.

Sometimes healing reveals a difficult truth:

One person is willing to grow.

The other is not.

When that happens, reconciliation may not be possible.

At that point, wisdom must guide the course.

A Captain's Perspective on Repair

When a vessel is damaged, the goal is usually restoration.

But restoration requires:

- honest inspection
- skilled labor
- time
- commitment
- cooperation

You cannot repair a hull while someone else drills new holes.

You cannot restore seaworthiness without shared effort.

Sometimes a vessel must be pulled from open water and placed in dry dock.

Engines cooled.
Damage assessed.
Corrosion addressed.

Temporary removal from sea does not mean abandonment.

It means preservation.

When the crew commits to restoration, a vessel can become stronger than before.

When only one person is working on the repair, wisdom must guide the course.

Hope is noble.

But navigation requires realism.

When Healing Leads to Reconciliation

Reconciliation is not a return to what was.

It is the creation of something new.

It requires:

- new language
- new boundaries
- new regulation

• new expectations
• new patterns

When done well, reconciliation does not recreate the old relationship.

It transforms it.

Sometimes the relationship that emerges after healing becomes far deeper than what existed before.

Because it is now built on awareness.
Not assumption.

On humility.
Not pride.

On safety.
Not fear.

The Invitation

If you are hoping for reconciliation, you are not naïve.

You are hopeful.

If you are doing the work while waiting, you are not weak.

You are courageous.

If you are discerning whether growth exists on both sides, you are not cynical.

You are wise.

Almost all relationships are redeemable when both hearts are willing.

When they are not, wisdom will guide you forward without bitterness and without shame.

Healing does not call you to abandon love.

It calls you to love from strength.

Not panic.
Not pride.
Not fear.
Strength.

True Healing Takes Time

Healing rarely moves as quickly as our emotions want it to, but clarity comes to those who are willing to slow down long enough to see truth.

CHAPTER 12

Anchored Hearts:

Living and Loving from Secure Love

Healing does not end with insight.

It ends with integration.

Insight is the moment you recognize your patterns.

Integration is the moment you begin living differently because of them.

Integration is quiet.

It does not announce itself.

It shows up in tone.
In pauses.
In steadiness under pressure.
In restraint where there once was reaction.

Integration is when the heart no longer just understands secure love — it begins to live from it.

This is what it means to have an anchored heart.

An Anchored Heart Is Not a Perfect Heart

An anchored heart still feels.

It still experiences disappointment.
It still encounters conflict.
It still gets triggered at times.
It still needs reassurance.
It still grows.

But it no longer drifts uncontrollably.

Anchors do not stop waves.

They stop drift.

Secure love does not eliminate difficulty.

It prevents panic from taking the wheel.

The difference between drifting and anchoring is not the absence of wind.

It is the discipline of remaining where you chose to anchor.

What Changes When the Heart Is Anchored

When healing takes root, the changes are often subtle—but powerful.

You begin to notice shifts like these:

• You pause more often.
• You react less intensely.
• You ask questions instead of assuming.
• You communicate more honestly.
• You repair more quickly.
• You rest more deeply.
• You tolerate uncertainty without catastrophe.

Fear may still knock, but it no longer moves in and rearranges the furniture.

Activation may still rise, but you do not automatically obey it.

Distance may still appear, but you do not instantly assume abandonment.

Your nervous system begins to recognize something new:

"This is uncomfortable."
"But I am not unsafe."

That distinction changes everything.

Guarding Against False Narratives

One of the greatest threats to anchored love is not conflict.

It is narrative distortion.

When attachment is activated — especially during distance, separation, or uncertainty — cognitive dissonance begins whispering stories.

"This isn't working."
"They never really cared."
"You were foolish to trust."
"You're incompatible."
"You're the only one trying."
"They're better off without you."

These narratives often feel convincing.

They feel protective.

They feel decisive.

However, many of them are fear seeking certainty.

Cognitive dissonance hates ambiguity.

It wants resolution.
It wants clarity.
It wants relief.

So, it simplifies complexity.

It turns struggle into incompatibility.
It turns activation into evidence.
It turns temporary distance into permanent rejection.

Anchored hearts slow down before believing the story.

They ask:

"What is actually true here?"
"What is fear amplifying?"
"What evidence do I truly have?"
"Is this reality — or reaction?"

Not Every Strong Feeling is the Voice of God

Sometimes it is fear looking for certainty.
Sometimes it is an old wound trying to protect itself.
Sometimes it is God gently inviting us toward truth.

God does not force our decisions.

He does not override our will, but He is not distant either.

He guides.
He convicts.
He invites.

Learning to discern the difference between His leading and our own internal reactions requires stillness, honesty, and time.

It requires us to slow down enough to ask:

"Is this peace — or urgency?"
"Is this wisdom — or fear?"
"Is this truth — or a story I am trying to resolve too quickly?"

For some, this confusion shows up in familiar patterns.

The anxious heart may feel urgency and call it direction.
"I need to fix this now."
"I need to reach out right now."
"I can't sit in this uncertainty."

The avoidant heart may feel relief and call it clarity.
"This is too much."
"I need space."
"This must not be right."

Both can feel convincing.
Both can feel certain.
But neither always reflects truth.

Anchored hearts learn not to move at the speed of activation.

They learn to pause.
To examine what is being felt.
To separate fear from wisdom.

They remember that God's voice does not rush them into panic and does not lead them away from truth.

Anchored hearts do not rush to label every impulse as direction.

They learn to wait, to examine, and to listen carefully before they move.

Anchored hearts do not deny pain.

They simply refuse distortion.

A Story of Holding Steady

Noah and Grace had reached a breaking point.

Arguments had become circular.
Both felt exhausted.
Both loved each other.
Both felt misunderstood.

They agreed to take space.

By day six, Noah's mind had built a case.

"She's done."
"She's tired of me."
"She's already moving on."

By day six, Grace had built her own narrative.

"He's relieved."
"He doesn't miss me."
"He never fought for us."

Both stories felt certain.

Both were incomplete.

Instead of deciding in isolation, they scheduled a mediated conversation.

When they sat down, neither came armed with accusations.

They came with questions.

"When you went quiet," Grace said softly, "my body told me I was alone."

"When things escalated," Noah replied, "my body told me I was failing you."

The story shifted.

They were not enemies.

They were activated.

Separation did not destroy their relationship.

Distortion nearly did.

Truth restored perspective.

Anchored love is not the absence of doubt.

It is the refusal to let doubt define reality without careful examination.

Do Not Give Up Too Quickly

This must be said clearly.

Do not give up on someone you love simply because fear is loud.

Do not abandon someone who is willing to grow simply because growth is uncomfortable.

Do not confuse struggle with disqualification.

Do not allow cognitive dissonance to convince you that something meaningful is meaningless.

Many relationships do not fail because love was absent.

They fail because fear was louder than truth.

Fear went unchecked.

Narratives went unchallenged.

Neither person slowed down long enough to seek clarity beneath activation.

So, look deeper.

Not into your anxiety.
Not into your pride.
Not into wounded memory.

Look into the present.

Is there humility on both sides?
Is there willingness?
Is there ownership?
Is there effort?
Is there growth — even if imperfect?

If the answer is yes, do not walk away lightly.

Anchored hearts fight wisely, not impulsively.

Loving Without Losing Yourself

Anchored love does not require self-erasure.

You can:

- love without fixing
- support without rescuing
- stay without overextending
- hope without denial
- pursue reconciliation without abandoning yourself

Security allows you to say:

"I want this relationship."
"I will not lose myself to keep it."

That is not selfishness.

That is integration.

Trusting God With the Outcome

One of the hardest lessons in secure living is releasing control over outcomes.

You can regulate yourself.
You can communicate honestly.
You can pursue repair.
You can seek help.

But you cannot force another person to grow.

Anchored hearts learn to say:

"I will show up with truth and humility, and I will trust God with what I cannot control."

Scripture reminds us:

"Trust in the Lord with all your heart and lean not on your own understanding."
— Proverbs 3:5–6

Anchored hearts trust not because life is predictable — but because God is faithful.

Trust does not eliminate effort.

It eliminates desperation.

Anchored Hearts Become Safe Places

Healed people love differently.

They lead differently.
They parent differently.
They partner differently.
They show up differently.

Anchored hearts become safe places.

Not because they never fail — but because they repair.

Not because they never doubt — but because they question distortion.

Not because they are perfect — but because they are grounded.

Safe people change lives.

They interrupt generational fear.

They model regulated presence.

They redefine love.

A Captain's Final Reflection

After decades on the water, one truth remains:

Storms are not optional.

They come suddenly.
They come repeatedly.
They come when you least expect them.

What determines survival is not the absence of storms.

It is whether the anchor holds when they arrive.

I have seen vessels damaged because captains panicked.

I have seen boats collide because crews reacted impulsively.

Often the greatest danger was not the weather — it was fear.

Anchors do not eliminate waves.

They prevent drift.

God's love is that anchor.

It held you when you were afraid.
It held you when you were confused.
It held you when you were triggered.

It holds you now.

It will hold you:

when conflict rises,
when separation tests you,
when doubt whispers,
when fear suggests surrender.

Anchored hearts do not drift into false narratives.

They return to truth.

You Are Anchored

You are not too much.

You are not broken beyond repair.

You are not foolish for hoping.

You are not weak for loving deeply.

You are healing.

As you continue walking with God — and with others — your heart will learn, again and again:

Love can be secure.

Connection can endure.

Fear does not have to lead.

Truth is worth seeking.

Reconciliation is worth fighting for when both hearts are willing.

Storms may rise.

But you are not drifting.

You are anchored.

A Closing Prayer

Father,

Thank You for meeting us in our wounds.
For staying when fear told us to run.
For loving us into wholeness.

Guard our hearts from distortion.
Anchor us in truth.

Give us courage to fight for love where growth exists.
Give us wisdom where release is required.

Heal what was broken.
Restore what can be restored.

Steady us when waves rise.
Teach us secure love.
Teach us anchored living.

In Jesus' name,
Amen

Epilogue

After the Storm

Every voyage changes a captain.

You leave the dock one way.
You return another.

Sometimes the difference is subtle.
Sometimes it is profound.

But the sea leaves its mark.

So does love.
So does loss.
So does healing.

If you have walked through these pages slowly, honestly, courageously — you are not the same person who began them.

Not because you mastered something.
Not because you solved everything.

But because you paused long enough to look beneath the surface.

That alone changes a life.

There was a time when I believed strength meant control.

Control of outcomes.
Control of emotions.
Control of the ship.
Control of the narrative.

But the sea has a way of humbling that illusion.

You cannot control the wind.
You cannot command the tide.
You cannot prevent every storm.

What you can do is prepare.

You can learn your vessel.
You can reinforce what is weak.
You can regulate your crew.
You can anchor wisely.

When the storm comes — because it will — you can choose not to panic.

That is secure love.

Not the absence of storms.

The refusal to let fear captain the ship.

If there is one thing I hope you carry forward, it is this:

Do not surrender to false narratives.

Not the ones fear whispers.
Not the ones pride constructs.
Not the ones cognitive dissonance fabricates in moments of distance and doubt.

When love feels tested, slow down.

Look deeper than the story your nervous system is telling.

Look beneath the activation.
Beneath the tension.
Beneath the silence.

Is there still humility?
Is there still effort?
Is there still growth?
Is there still willingness?

If there is, do not walk away lightly.

Almost all relationships are salvageable when both hearts are willing.

That conviction is not naïve.

It is anchored.

But hear this too:

Anchored does not mean trapped.

Secure love does not endure abuse.
It does not excuse cruelty.
It does not ignore chronic refusal.

Wisdom and hope must walk together.

Strength and tenderness must coexist.

Sometimes the most anchored thing you can do
is release without bitterness
and move forward without shame.

Even that can be redemptive.

Over the years, I have seen boats that should have sunk.

Hulls cracked and corroded.
Engines strained and worn.
Crews exhausted and unheard.

Because someone was willing to inspect honestly, repair patiently, and commit fully.

Those vessels sailed again.

Not because they avoided damage.
Because they addressed it.

That is what healing does.

It does not pretend nothing happened.
It rebuilds differently.

If you are reading this in a season of uncertainty, hear me clearly:

Do not give up too quickly.

Not on yourself.
Not on the one you love.
Not on growth.
Not on love that still shows signs of life.

Look deeply.

Truth lives beneath fear.
Humility lives beneath defensiveness.
Desire for connection often lives beneath withdrawal.

Slow down long enough to see clearly.

Anchored hearts do not react impulsively.

They examine carefully.

If you are reading this in a season of stability, guard it well.

Security is built in repetition.

Continue pausing.
Continue repairing.
Continue choosing regulation over reaction.
Continue trusting God with what you cannot control.

Your anchors are not dramatic.

They are steady.

Above all, remember this:

God is not fragile.

His presence does not disappear when you struggle.
His love does not withdraw when you activate.
His steadiness does not fluctuate with your fear.

He is the anchor beneath every other anchor.

When everything feels uncertain,
He remains.

One day, after this book is closed, you will face another storm.

You may feel the wind rise.
You may feel old patterns stir.
You may feel doubt begin its familiar whisper.

When that happens, take that sacred pause.

Breathe.

Remember what you learned.

You are not powerless.
You are not drifting.
You are not alone.

You are anchored.

Anchored hearts weather storms not because they are unbreakable — but because they are held.

If this book has done anything worthwhile,
I hope it has helped you anchor more deeply.

In truth.
In humility.
In courage.
In reconciliation where possible.
In wisdom where necessary.
In God above all.

The sea will not grow quieter.

But you can grow steadier.

Believe me when I say that changes everything.

Before you set this book down, let me leave you with one final thought.

Anchored hearts are not formed in comfort.

They are formed in questions.
In prayers that feel unanswered.
In conversations that stretch us beyond what feels safe.
In moments when we must decide whether fear will steer — or whether we will slow down long enough to listen for truth.

Every storm has the potential to teach us something about the condition of our vessel.

Some storms reveal damage.

Some storms reveal strength.

Most storms reveal both.

What matters most is not that the sea becomes calm, but that we learn where our anchor truly rests.

If your heart has felt unsteady, if your relationships have carried confusion, if you have wondered whether healing is really possible, hear this clearly:

God is not finished with you.

He is not discouraged by your questions.
He is not surprised by your fear.
He is not distant from your story.

The same God who steadies oceans is fully capable of steadying hearts.

The same love that anchors us to Him can teach us, patiently and faithfully, how to love others with courage, humility, and grace.

So, keep learning.
Keep repairing.
Keep listening.
Keep choosing truth over fear.

Because anchored hearts do not drift forever.

They learn where home is.

The story that shaped this book is not about blame. It was written because of two people who loved deeply while carrying wounds they did not yet understand.

If this book resonated with you, consider sharing it with someone who may also be navigating questions about love, fear, and healing.

If the message of *Anchored Hearts* helped you see your own story with greater clarity, leaving a short review helps other readers discover it as well.

— Capt. Tony —

Acknowledgments

I am grateful to the people who encouraged this work long before it became a manuscript.

To the friends who listened while I processed difficult lessons.

To those who read early drafts and offered honest feedback.

To the friends, family, counselors, pastors, authors, social media voices, and teachers whose work on attachment theory, healing, and faith helped shape my understanding.

Tom, Joe, Brandon, Ashley, Michelle N., Kara, Taylr, Michelle B., David J., Wayne S., Brad, Ray, Al, Wayne K., Evan, Bree, David N., Jennifer, Amanda, Kurt, Tim, Christina, Shannon, Jadyn, Amee, Miguel, and so many more. I can't thank you enough for your listening, discussion, reading, counseling, and support.

Finally, to the many people who quietly carry attachment wounds while continuing to seek healing, you inspired far more of this book than you realize.

This book exists because of the grace of God and the patience of many people.

This journey is not finished for me either. As of this writing, I am still hurting deeply, still learning, still growing, still healing, and still being shaped along the way. I still love her and miss her every single day. I probably will for the rest of my life.

— ⚓ —

About the Author

Capt. Tony Newberry is a lifelong mariner based in Wilmington, North Carolina, where he owns and operates Island Cruises in nearby Carolina Beach. Over the course of his maritime career, he has captained a wide variety of vessels around the world, including cruise ships, crewboats, party cruise boats, head boats, offshore support vessels, core sample drill ships, tow boats, and tugs.

Anchored Hearts was born out of a deeply personal season of emotional pain following the breakup with the love of his life. While searching for understanding and healing, Tony discovered attachment theory — a concept he had never encountered before — and began studying it extensively. As he explored the intersection of attachment, emotional healing, and faith, he felt a strong calling to help others navigate similar storms in their own lives.

With Christian faith as his foundation, Tony believes that true healing comes through both honest self-understanding and the steady love of God. *Anchored Hearts* reflects that journey.

When he is not writing or working on the water, Tony enjoys travel, learning, mentoring others, and helping people navigate life's storms with steadiness and faith.

Future resources, including small-group and workbook materials designed to accompany *Anchored Hearts*, are being developed to help individuals, couples, and ministries explore these ideas more deeply.

For updates and additional resources, visit:
www.anchoredheartsministry.com

www.ingramcontent.com/pod-product-compliance
Lightning Source LLC
LaVergne TN
LVHW090516110826
845146LV00003B/882

* 9 7 9 8 9 9 5 3 1 2 0 0 0 *